# The London and North Western Railway around Preston

# EUXTON, FARINGTON & PRESTON.

1913

From Fleetwood
LEA ROAD
Fr. Lancaster
OXHEYS
To Longridge
GREEN BANK SID.
P.&W. GOODS (MAUDLANDS)
P.&W. GOODS BRCH JN.
DEEPDALE PASS.
JUNCTION
2m 45c
36c
30c
11c
0m 68c
24c
33c
DEEPDALE GOODS
RIBBLE BRANCH
1m 29c
1m 30c
DOCK
P.&W. JUNC.
19c
P.&L. JUNC.
10c
14c
DOCK STREET JN.
PRESTON
STRAND ROAD JUNCTION
JOINT PASS. & JN. (FISHERGATE)
BUTLER STREET GOODS (L.&Y.)
CHRISTIAN ROAD GOODS (L.&N.W.)
39c
W. LANCS. STA. GOODS
JUNC.
R. RIBBLE
RIBBLE JUNCTION
PENWORTHAM JUNCTION
0m 26c
22c
28c
23c
28c
WHITEHOUSE JUNC.
MIDDLEFORTH JUNC.
1m 24c
32c
From Southport
FARINGTON WEST JUNC.
8c
0m 74c
PRESTON JN. STA. JUNCTION
BAMBER BRIDGE STA.
To Blackburn
9c
0m 49c
JUNCTION
17c
1m 1c
0m 57c
0m 58c
23c
7c
0m 46c
JUNC.
MOSS LANE JUNC.
55c PASS
30c
BOSTOCK HALL STA.
EAST JUNC.
GOODS JUNC.
20c
18c
45c
1m 60c
FARINGTON
MIDGE HALL
LEYLAND
1m 33c
From Liverpool
1m 34c

## EXPLANATION
CORPORATION OF PRESTON
LANCASHIRE & YORKSHIRE
LONDON & NORTH WESTERN
L.&Y. & L.&N.W. JOINT { NORTH UNION / PRN. & LONGRIDGE / PRESTON & WYRE }
N. UNION & CORPORATION JOINT

EUXTON
JUNCTION 12c
L.&Y. STA.
To Bolton
To Wigan
1m 24c
BALSHAW LANE & EUXTON

# The London and North Western Railway around Preston

*A history of the 'North Union' at Preston station and the lines to Bolton, Fleetwood, Lancaster, Longridge and Wigan, including the Dock Branch and Lancaster Canal*

## Bob Gregson

ATKINSON
PUBLICATIONS LTD

# Dedicated to the railwaymen and women
# of Preston past and present

Cover illustrations:

Front cover:    Lostock Hall Black 5, 44971, shunts passenger stock in the final days of
                steam traction. *(G.V. Sharpe)*

Back cover:     Top, L.N.W.R. official postcard, looking north along platform 5. *(Author's collection)*
                Bottom, Aerial photo of the Fishergate end of Preston station, circa 1920.
                *(British Railways Board)*

Frontispiece:   A 1913 diagram of Preston area junctions
                as published for the Railway Clearing House.

First published July 2012

Atkinson Publications Limited
PO Box 688, Preston,
Lancashire PR3 8AX
www.atkinsonspublications.co.uk

British Library Cataloguing in Publication Data.
A catalogue record for this book is available from the British Library.

ISBN 978 1 909134 02 7

Typesetting and Origination by Atkinson Publications Limited.
Printed and bound by CPI Group (UK) Ltd, Croydon, CR0 4YY

# Contents

# Acknowledgements

I would like to take this opportunity to thank the following people for all their help without which the completion of this book would not have been possible.

Heather Crook, Margaret Heyes, Adrian Bradshaw, Mike & Paul Atherton, Bob Tye, John Fletcher, Paul Tuson, Stan Withers, Jack Hodgkinson, Alan Castle, Bill Ashcroft, Jim Heron, David Hindle, Chris Spring, Arthur Haymes, Richard Kirkby, Frank Herdman, Paul Gregson, Richard Parker, Dr. David Hunt of the South Ribble Museum, Leyland, Mike Norris, Mel Parker, Jeff Mimnagh, Ken Roberts, David Hunt, Bernard Bond, Andy Hall, Eric (Tom) Jones, Pete Whalen, Bob Gant, Vinny & John Commons, Brian Dodds, Walter (Rocky) Thompson, Ben Brooksbank, Ted (Jacko) Jackson, Bryan Daggers, David Dyson, Jim Marlor, Jim Walker, David & Sylvie Holmes, David Whitehead, Fred Jackson, Hilary Snape, Dennis Westwood, Tommy Gorman, Norman Bullcock, Tony Gillett, Irene Sergeant, Peter Rigby, Barry Frankland, David Burdon, Colin Stacey, E. H. Wood, J .S. Hancock, Malcolm Baker, Paul Wood, Brian Southworth, Billy Wilson, Ronnie Clough, Jeff Ford, John Rigby and many other Preston and Lostock Hall railwaymen, too numerous to mention.
The Harris Library and Museum, Lancashire Records Office, Greater Manchester Records Office, The National Railway Museum, National Grid Archives, National Records Office, British Railways Board, Lancashire County Council, Lancashire Evening Post, South Ribble Museum, Leyland Library, Leyland Historical Society, British Railways Residuals.

A proud driver and his engine. Tony Gillett with Black 5, 44767, on February 11, 1961 at Liverpool Exchange. I am indebted to Tony for allowing me to use some of his superb photographs in this book. Thankfully he took his camera with him wherever he went on the railway. *(Tony Gillett Archive)*

# Foreword

Back in the 1960's, during my wanderings around Preston, it never occurred to me just how many companies were involved in the creation of its railway system, for I was too preoccupied with what was going on in that decade of decline. It was a race against time to catch a glimpse of the steam workings before they all disappeared in 1968. I was still at school (or assumed to have been at any rate) in those final years, and not having the means with which to travel far, I came to regard Preston as the 'poor man's Crewe'; but it wasn't all that poor by a long way, as I did manage to see off the last of the Stanier Pacifics, Scots, Patriots, Jubilees, Crabs and Super D's. By the time my pals and I were able to get further afield, Preston engine shed had already been closed, and was being used as a storage point for redundant steam locomotives. It was now possible to get round the place without being thrown out but, although we could climb up into the cabs, mess around with the controls, and play at being engine drivers, there was something of the graveyard about the place, and it was quite daunting to know that all those fine engines were destined for the breaker's yard. We had various favourite places where we could watch the activity without getting into bother. There was the 'Glass Bridge' at the south end of the station, and the coal yard at Maudland, Vicar's Bridge on the E.L.; the junction fork at Bee Lane etc. No day out was complete without a visit to the docks, where we were guaranteed a footplate ride on one of the saddle tanks. I always came away from that place with a headache and a feeling of nausea, after being subjected to obnoxious Diesel exhaust fumes from the ships' donkey engines near by. Give me coal smoke and steam any day!! It was good to cycle up to Garstang & Catterall station on a fine day, and wait for the 'Pilling Pig' to arrive from Preston. The engine was usually a Black 5 from Lostock Hall shed, and the train would normally wait for some time at the station before moving on up the branch. The station master there was a decent chap, and didn't bother about us hanging about near the footbridge, so long as we kept clear of the platform edges. He would even come out and tell us which train was passing next and the likely form of motive power. We had no idea of working timetables etc. in those days, we simply kept our eyes on the signals, willing the arm to go in the 'Off' position. The problem with being in that particular location was, that on some occasions, we missed numbers as the passenger trains came thundering through at such high-speeds. They were idyllic days, and I can still sense the warm aroma of pitch pine and the Aeolian melody of the breeze in the telegraph wires.

The central station at Preston was always an uncomfortable place to be, if you didn't happen to be there for the purpose of going on a journey. Certain members of staff would tell us to go away, or words to that effect, and if we didn't, they would call in a Transport Policeman or two. The platforms had been surfaced with a non-slip asphalt, and the old four-wheeled parcels trolleys with iron wheels had been replaced by lighter types with pneumatic rubber tyres, and were pulled along by battery-powered tractor units. They were completely noiseless amid the general hub hub of the station, and you had to be on the look out for them, as the drivers never took prisoners. They would whip round from behind a building at speed, and steer straight for us with murder in their eyes; we were, therefore, obliged to dodge out of the way quick-sharp, or else. Throughout its notorious history, the station had never been a pleasant place on which to spend any great length of time, especially on a dark, cold Winter's evening, when an icy wind blew straight through it. We never got bothered with staff in the evenings, and when waiting for the train home, a south-bound parcels train would arrive at No. 5 platform, and we would wander down to the southernmost block, past a mountain of mailbags to take a look at the engine. Men were busy loading up the new 'Brute Cages' [1] with mail bags and parcels and wheeling them into the coaches. It was here that I noticed the two brass plaques on doors either side of the building, commemorating the free station buffets which operated during both world wars. They were caked in green verdigris and barely legible, but It was from these forgotten relics that I gained the inspiration to investigate further into the history of the station. How time used to linger on those dark nights. It was like a monochrome movie from the 1920's, no colour, just shades of grey and black shadows. Those waiting on the platform resembled blackened stone statues, standing there dumb and lifeless until the train arrived, and then a transformation occurred. It was lighter and much warmer in those DMU carriages, and as the people boarded the train, they became living creatures again, animated, colourful and communicative. It was as though they had awakened from hibernation.

1966 saw the introduction of Inter-City and the corporate blue livery on locomotives and stock. The proud lion was being phased out and replaced by the 'Keep right and left' sign. The new fluorescent lighting on the platforms, the diffusers of which bore the station's name in red capitals, did little or nothing to relieve the overall gloomy aspect of the place; and piped music was coming over the P.A. system to soothe the anxieties of those whose trains were running late – or not at all. I well remember taking a close look at Black 5, 45149, which was on Pilot duty one evening in November, 1967. She was at the top end of what is now platform 3, waiting for the London-Glasgow train to arrive. The driver was taking it easy with both feet on the regulator handle, and the fireman was lost in a newspaper. It presented a scene of domestic fireside bliss, enhanced by the relaxing notes of Hoagy Carmichael's Stardust. That tune still haunts me to this day!

I have fond memories of the later years, and the quiet Saturday afternoon chats in the Boatman's pub at the top end of Marsh Lane, where I would listen to stories about the many characters who had frequented the pub over the decades; such tales as came from enginemen, shunters, canal boat skippers, wharfingers, coal merchants and carters, who gathered together in the pub at the end of the day to wash down the dust with good, strong ale. They were mostly rough and ready characters with loud voices, who enjoyed a bit of banter, a friendly argument and a good laugh. The atmosphere would have been thick with a variety of occupational and habitual odours, including the earthly smell of coal; horse sweat and leather aprons; hot potato pies, beer fumes and tobacco smoke, which would rise up in clouds, leaving a mustardy tint on the ceilings. I used to call in around noon after work on a Saturday, and Barbara would knock up a couple of roast beef and onion barms, which I eagerly scoffed and washed down with a couple of jars of extra-stout. I used to sit in the left corner of the bar near the kitchen, where the strong shafts of sunlight entered obliquely through the frosted glass window, throwing everything else into shadow. The landlord, Alex Heaton, would reflect on those bygone Saturday nights in the wintertime, when the locals gathered in the snug by a blazing fire and sang old-time medleys to the accompaniment of a Victorian upright piano. Those cheerful social gatherings faded away when the communities were cleared out, split up and distributed to other parts of the town, their homes giving place to the monstrosities we see today. The day-time trade from Ladywell House ebbed away following B.R.'s decision to prohibit all their staff from entering licensed premises during working hours. The Boatman's was more like a museum than a pub; one of those old-fashioned places where everything on display had a story attached to it. The walls were adorned with old maritime pictures and artefacts; there were model ships here and there and a remarkable display of Guinness ornaments behind the bar. I was always sensitive of a surpassingly strange atmosphere in that place which cannot be adequately described; it could only be sensed in the half gloom and pervading twilight by those of a meditative nature. It was one of those rare places, where time is transformed into space, providing a peaceful refuge from the sound and fury of the hideous modern world without. It was unlooked for and found by chance; it presented a haven soon to vanish. It's gone now, and in its place stands a hideous, steel-framed box without a soul.

The memories of those years live on, and It has been my privilege to have talked to the railwaymen and women of Preston, many of whom are now, at the time of writing, in their 70's - 90's. Without their valuable assistance, I would not have been able to present a work of this magnitude. I have not introduced the early railway companies in their chronological order of arrival, as there was a need to keep things together, somewhat, where the Lancaster Canal Company was involved.

Bob Gregson.
June 2012

Disclaimer.
*Whilst every effort has been made to track down photographic sources (most of them successfully), there are one or two images which I have had in my possession for many years and for which I have no basic or adequate data to work on.*

# FOOTNOTES

[1] Brute cages (British Rail Universal Trolley Equipment) were introduced on the Western Region in 1964, and were soon in use at all large stations around the country. They had two fixed wheels aft. And two swivelling wheels forward, couplings at either end and a brake pin. They were fitted with steel mesh on three sides and the one open side was fitted with lugs for fixing canvas sheets across to keep the contents secure. They all fell into disuse following the withdrawal of the parcels and mail services in 1990.

# CHAPTER ONE

# The Arrival of the Railways in Preston

## North Union Railway

On April 22, 1831, an act was passed for the construction of a line from Wigan to Preston. By 1833, however, the company was still struggling to raise the necessary capital, and the board unanimously recommended an amalgamation with the Wigan Branch Railway. This was duly carried out, and the North Union Railway, as it became known, was given Royal assent on May 22, 1834 and became the first such railway amalgamation to be sanctioned by Parliament. Contracts were tendered for in January 1835, and the much awaited work on the 15 ½ mile line began. W. B. Vignoles was appointed chief engineer for the line, and John Collister was the company's resident engineer. Vignoles was later to become chief engineer for the N.U. in June, 1834 at a salary of £1,200 per annum.[1]

The work was divided into three contracts, with Henry, Mullins & McMahon at the Preston end, covering a length of 2 ½ miles from the terminus to a point just to the south of Farington, at a cost of £80,000; William Mackenzie of Liverpool, on the centre section, or Yarrow contract, from Farington to Coppull Summit, a distance of 8 miles at a cost of £52,589, and William Hughes of Glasgow, on the Douglas contract from Coppull to Chapel Lane in Wigan, a distance of 5 miles at a cost of £60,000.

## COAL CINDERS
## NORTH UNION RAILWAY

Persons having Cinders
to dispose of in large quantities
will be treated
with for the purchase
and delivery thereof,
by applying to
Messrs. HENRY MULLINS
and MACMAHON,
at their office in
Butler Street, Preston

November 10th, 1835.

*Preston Chronicle, 14 November, 1835.*

Charles Blacker Vignoles.
*(Author's collection)*

The only serious problem to occur during the course of construction was the collapse of a double culvert on the River Yarrow on Sunday, October 22, 1837. The culvert was 101 yards in length with two arches, each having a span of 20ft., the embankment above being 65 ft in height. At noon, some 30 yards of the culvert fell in and completely blocked the passage of water. Over 150 men were brought in to remove tons of earth and masonry, and local farmers were busy trying to save as much of their crops (mainly potatoes) as they could. Heavy downpours added to the problems and the surrounding fields began to flood quickly; 150 aces of meadow and pasture land became inundated and some of the adjoining fields were under 25ft. of water. Some days later, a 3-arched brick bridge carrying a road over the N.U. collapsed. As a temporary measure, the embankment (400,000 cubic yards) was cut back and replaced by a 400ft. long timber trestle, with a height of 73 ft. It was deemed that the foundations of the culvert had not been set down far enough and had not been strong enough to withstand the weight of earth above them. The embankment slopes had been set out at 2 ½ to 1, but on account of the yielding nature of the clay, they had slipped to 3 ½ to 1. A new culvert was constructed, in January

1855, the work being carried out by Henry, Mullins & McMahon at a cost of £50,000.

On September 1, 1835, one of the N.U. Directors, William Taylor, ceremoniously laid the foundation stone for what was to become the most prominent and graceful structure on the line, the Ribble bridge. A large crowd of spectators looked on, and such was the curiosity and enthusiasm to see the construction work in progress that, by March, 1836, the contractors had to respectfully announce that no persons could be admitted within the palings erected around the site without a certificate of admission. The only serious set-back occurred on June 30, 1837, when a severe gale brought down the timber centering for the first arch (Preston side). The total length of this magnificent structure is 872 ft. and the original width (for double track) was 28 ft. It has a height of 68 ft. from the bed of the river to the top of the parapet, and the high-water mark to the keystone of each arch is 50 ft. There are 5 elliptical arches, each having a span of 120 ft. and brick relieving arches are located in the spaces between the main arches in order to diminish the superincumbent pressure and to divert the weight upon the piers. The versed sine of each arch is 33 ft. and the depth of the arch stones is 10 ft. diminishing to 5 ft. at the key. The abutments are 30 ft. thick and the one on the north side of the river is 18 ft. in depth from its base to the springer. The abutment on the south side is 28 ft. deep and the wing walls are 67 ft. in length, resting upon piles from 11 to 16 ft. in depth. The piers are 20 ft. thick and average 22 ft. from their foundations. The parapet is 2 ft. thick and is 4 ½ ft. in height from the top of the rails. The whole is constructed of rusticated ashlar and comprises 670,000 cubic feet of stone, raised from the quarries at Lancaster, Whittle and Longridge.

The bridge was designed by W.B. Vignoles, and the work was carried out by Henry, Mullins & McMahon of Dublin at a cost of £40,000. Because of its estimated cost of construction, the N.U. was given authority to charge pontage. The height of the adjoining southern embankment is 40 ft. and has a length of three quarters of a mile. The base has a width of 190 ft. and the slope is a steep 2 to 1. It contains 484, 431 cubic yards of earth, most of which came from the Penwortham cutting. In 1836, Vignoles took a model of the bridge to Ireland and showed it to the Society of Civil Engineers, who agreed that it was almost identical to John Rennie's Waterloo bridge of 1817, the only noticeable differences being that it had five arches instead of nine, and that the parapet comprised blocks instead of balusters. The original plan had been for a 12 arch bridge with iron spans.

A north-bound freight crosses the Ribble bridge around the turn of the century. *(Author's collection)*

North Union embankment
from Miller Park.
*(Winter & Kidson)*

The total amount of rock, sand, marl and earth excavated was 2,202,030 cubic yards, and the total amount of excavations used in the construction of embankments was 2,118,498 cubic yards. 3,000 men were at work on the line with a further 300 having been employed in the final stages of construction. The cost of the line amounted to £21,000 per mile, including engines and carriages. Vignoles insisted that stone blocks be used to carry the rails at 4 ft. intervals in cuttings, and wooden sleepers at the same distance on embankments with a height of 6 ft. or over. The ballast for both types comprised sand on a base of broken stones, gravel and cinders. The rails were made of wrought or malleable iron and were supplied in lengths of 12 to 16 ft. [2]

Following the completion of intermediate stations at Farington, Golden Hill (later named Leyland), Euxton (later replaced by Balshaw Lane), Coppull and Standish, the line was inspected in October, 1838, and on Sunday, the 21st day of that month, a special director's train, comprising a Bury type engine, and a single coach, ran the full length of the line from Preston to the junction with the Liverpool & Manchester at Parkside and back, without stopping at Wigan. The locomotive was No. 2, built by Jones, Turner & Evans at their Viaduct Foundry, Earlestown near Newton-le-Willows. The official opening of the line for passengers and goods came 10 days later when a train of 5 carriages carrying 29 passengers including the resident engineer, Mr. Collister, left Preston for a return journey to Parkside at 7 a.m. The locomotive was the same one that had been used for the directors. A local correspondent gave a prosaic description of the locomotive as she departed from Preston: *"She hissed and boiled like Phlegathon and scattered her cinders like the volcanic crater of Aetna".*

Speed was reduced as the train approached the Ribble bridge, owing to work on the structure still in progress. Farington was reached in ten minutes and Golden Hill station in a quarter of an hour. The train stopped here to allow a Captain Pollard to get on board, then set off again for Euxton station, which was reached in nine minutes, where the train stopped again to collect another gentleman by the name of Mr. R. Alison, from Charnock, who was deposited among the first class travellers. The train ran well and reached a speed of 30 mph through the Yarrow Valley, which was probably the fastest most of those on board had ever travelled. There was a scheduled stop at Spendmore but, owing to an oversight on the part of the guard, it went straight through. The train arrived in Wigan to a ten-gun salute, and remained there for around five minutes before setting off for the junction at Parkside. The 22 mile journey had been made in an hour and a quarter.

Earliest known photograph of Farington Station in North Union days. *(Harris Library)*

The return journey was somewhat delayed, due to a number of heavy wheels and axles having been loaded onto the luggage wagon, and the locomotive having developed a fault which slowed it down considerably. The 1 in 100 gradient between Mr. Rylance's factory and the Boar's head proved too much for the ailing engine, and passengers were obliged to get out and push the train up the hill. Other travellers called for horse-drawn carriages and dismissed the new railway as a waste of time. A second train hauled by engine No. 5, which had been built by Hicks of Bolton, fared much better and the return journey from Wigan to Preston was completed in 27 minutes. This was the 8 45 a.m. first class from Preston with Sir Peter Hesketh Fleetwood, Baronet on board, which set off from Parkside at around 10 30 a.m., with one carriage from Liverpool and two from Manchester. A crowd had gathered at Wigan station where church bells were ringing and flags flying, with a large red example on the station roof bearing the legend, 'The Queen and her Glorious Constitution.' From Wigan the Yarrow viaduct was reached in 15 minutes, with the train now averaging 36 mph. Golden Hill was passed three minutes later and the south end of the Ribble bridge in seven. The train arrived in Preston to a magnificent reception of bells, flags, bands playing and loud and protracted cheers from the thousands of spectators.

Busy scene at Farington Junction. *(Authors Collection)*

At 11 a.m., engine No. 5 left Preston for Wigan with the company secretary, Mr. Chapman, the resident engineer, Mr. Collister, William Taylor and John Winstanley. The train returned in an hour and a half, hauling two wagon-loads of coal and one of cannel, which had been brought down the newly opened Springs Branch from Haigh to Wigan. A flag had been set up on one of the wagons, bearing an image of a coach and horses turned upside down with the motto, 'No imposition to Wigan.' At half past two in the afternoon, a mixed train left Preston with 110 passengers, by far the largest number of people to be carried on the N.U. that day, and the last train to leave Preston on that momentous day comprised first class carriages only and was hauled by the company's No. 4 engine. It departed at 4 45 p.m. and returned from Parkside at 6 45.

A company of directors from the Liverpool end arrived at Preston around 6 p.m. on a train hauled by the No. 2 engine, Those on board included Hardman Earle, Joseph Hornby, Benjamin Thomas, Joseph Ewart and Reece Bevan. They had been invited to dinner that evening by the Lord Mayor of Preston, Thomas German, along with directors from the Preston end, namely William Taylor, John Winstanley, William Calrow and Charles Swainson. Other distinguished guests included Sir Peter Hesketh Fleetwood, Bart, M.P., T.B Addison, Recorder of Preston; Charles Vignoles, the engineer in chief; Mr. Collister, Mr. McMahon, one of the contractors; Mr. Chapman, the secretary; the Rev. J. Clay, and William Clayton.

Black 5, No. 44873, passes beneath the East Lancashire line with a fast southbound train on July 1, 1962. (G. W. Sharpe)

Leyland station and goods shed in the early 1970's. *(Leyland Historical Society)*

Leyland station looking north. *(Leyland Historical Society)*

Leyland station booking office and station master's house in the 1970's. *(Leyland Historical Society)*

South of Skew Bridge. Britannia Pacific, 70009 Alfred the Great passes class 5, 44669 with a Barrow-Crewe express in 1966. *(Courtesy, Walter Thompson)*

44676 passes Skew Bridge with a local train in the mid 60's. *(Stan Withers)*

There were only four locomotives in operation at that time, with No's 6 and 7 in the process of being constructed by Hicks of Bolton, who had already built No's 4 and 5. The driving wheels of these engines were 5ft. 6 ins. in diameter, and the fore-wheels, 4 ft; the cylinders had a diameter of 12 ins. with an 18 ins. stroke. The boilers contained 62 tubes, each with a diameter of 2 ins. and had a maximum steam pressure of 70 pounds per square inch. The weight upon the driving wheels was 5 tons, 18 cwt., and 4 tons, 12 cwt. on the smaller wheels. The tenders had a capacity of 730 gallons of water and 15 cwt. of coal. The company also owned 15 first and 15 second class carriages, of which four of the first class were built by Dunn & Wise of Lancaster, having the Birmingham Arms at one end, the London Arms at the other and the Preston and Wigan in the centre. They were of an improved plan, with the seat divisions being carried up to the roof. Four more carriages were built by Messrs. Leece & Co. of Preston, the buffing being finished in the style of the L&M stock with that company's Arms at each end and the Preston & Wigan Arms on the centre door. Another four carriages were made by Jonathan Dunn & Son of Lancaster, and another three by Dawson's of Dublin. Nine of the second class were made by Dunn & Wise of Lancaster, where buffing was after the plan of those on the Grand Junction Railway, and another six were built by Penny's of Butler Street, Preston, with the buffing in the style of the L&M.

LNW 4-6-0, 1782, with a mixed freight south of Farington Curve Junction. *(H. Gordon Tidy)*

| Timetable and Particulars for N.U.R. October 31, 1838. | | | |
|---|---|---|---|
| | £ | s | d |
| First class coach, whether in first class or mixed train. | 0 | 7 | 6 |
| Second class mixed carriage. | 0 | 5 | 0 |
| Children under ten years of age, first class. | 0 | 4 | 0 |
| Children under ten years of age, second class. | 0 | 2 | 6 |
| Infants in arms. | Free | | |
| Gentleman's carriages, 4 wheels. | 1 | 0 | 0 |
| Gentleman's carriages, 2 wheels. | 1 | 0 | 0 |
| Two horses in the same box, belonging to the same owner. | 1 | 4 | 0 |
| As above, for three horses. | 1 | 8 | 0 |
| One horse. | 0 | 12 | 6 |

| Table for trains travelling between Preston, Liverpool, Manchester and Wigan. | | |
|---|---|---|
| From Preston to Liverpool or Manchester. | From Liverpool to Preston. | From Manchester to Preston. |
| 7.0 a.m. Mixed | 7.15 a.m. Mixed | 7.30 a.m. Mixed |
| 8.45 a.m. First Class | 9.0 a.m. First Class | 9.15 a.m. First Class |
| 2.30 p.m. Mixed | 2.45 p.m. Mixed | 3.0 p.m. Mixed |
| 5.45 p.m. First Class | 5.0 p.m. First Class | 5.15 p.m. First Class |

# NORTH UNION RAILWAY.

## To Masons, Builders & others.

Persons willing to Tender for the Erection and Completion of the Offices, &c., Coach House and Sheds, on the Preston Station of the North Union Railway, may see the Plans and Specifications prepared for the same by applying at the Office of the Company, in Cannon Street, Preston, from Monday the 22nd to Wednesday the 31st instant. Tenders to be delivered in sealed, addressed to "James Chapman, Esq., *Secretary to the North Union Railway Company, Harrington Street, Liverpool.*" and endorsed "*Tender for Preston Station,*" on or before Thursday the 1st February. Further Particulars may be obtained by applying to James Chapman, Esq., at the Office of the Company, Liverpool, or to Mr. F. W. Tuson, Architect, Cannon Street, Preston.

Preston Chronicle, 18 January, 1878.

Mixed trains only travelled on Sundays with a reduced service of just one in the morning and one in the evening. The morning train left Preston at 6 30; Liverpool and Manchester trains left at 7 0; the evening trains left Preston at 5 0; Liverpool and Manchester trains left at 5 30.

From Preston to London and Birmingham, the first class train left Preston at 8 45 a.m. and connected with the Grand Junction at Newton Bridge at 10 0 a.m.; the 2 30 p.m. proceeded from Newton Bridge at 5 0 p.m. and the 4 45 p.m. left Newton Bridge at 6 30 p.m. Trains from Birmingham to Preston left at 6 0 a.m. (mixed stock) and connected with the N.U. at Newton Bridge at 3 30 p.m., and the 11 30 a.m. was ready for departure from Newton Bridge at 5 30 p.m.

The first class trains carried six persons only in each carriage, and stopped at Euxton Lane and Wigan. The mixed trains consisted of both first and second class carriages and stopped at all the stations on the N.U. and L&M railways. There were strict rules pertaining to passengers and luggage. The doors to the booking office were to be closed precisely at the time of the train's departure, and booked tickets for first class travellers were numbered to correspond with the number of the seat taken. Carpet bags and small luggage were to be stowed beneath the seats opposite to where the owners were sitting; larger items of luggage were to be secured on the carriage roofs or in the boots. All persons were requested to get into and alight from the coaches invariably from the left side, as the only certain means of preventing accidents from trains passing in the opposite direction.

Only the company's porters were allowed to load and unload the luggage and place it upon any omnibus or cart at the stations, and no fees or gratuities were allowed to be paid to the guards, porters or any other employees of the company.[3] There was a smoking ban in the first class carriages and no person was allowed to sell liquor or eatables along the line. A minimum charge of one shilling was applied to parcels, and a memo from the company secretary, James Chapman, declared that the Branch Railway to New Springs, in the townships of Haigh and Aspul, commonly called New Springs Branch, was to be opened for passengers and goods at the same time.

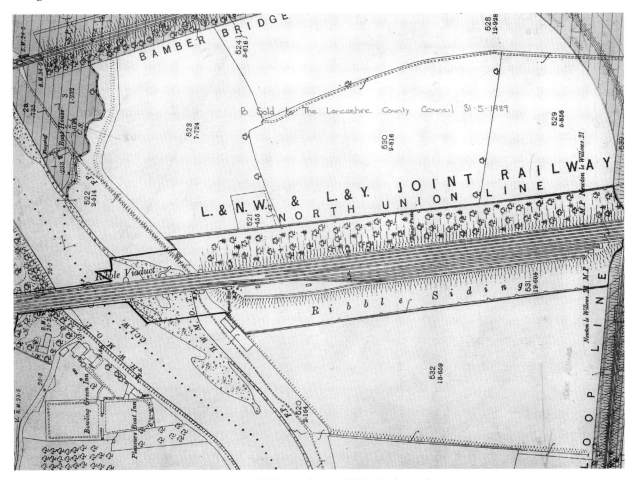

Plan of Ribble Sidings. *(BRB Residuals)*

The passenger station at Preston had two platforms, terminating at Fishergate, and right from the beginning it was considered to be inadequate for the volume of traffic which was steadily increasing on a weekly basis; indeed, as early as 1848, a government inspector concluded that the station was *"Utterly insufficient for the traffic passing through it."* It was designed by the Liverpool architect, Mr. J. Tuach and constructed of stone on the Italian style. A similar design was drawn up for the station at Wigan. The train shed was covered by a timber and iron roof, measuring 120 ft. in length by 40 ft. in width. The adjacent goods station was 180 ft. long by 125 ft. wide, and was specially designed for the transshipment of timber. The roof comprised four longitudinal gables, supported within the walls by three rows of iron columns at 20 ft. centres. The tubular columns also served as rainwater down spouts and some of them were fitted with jib-cranes. The principle rafters were reinforced with iron plates and the roof was partially glazed. The premises were let out to John Hargreaves, who was contracted to handle the goods traffic, using his own engines. The coal sidings were conveniently placed for the construction of a coal-drop to the low-level yard adjacent to Syke Street. The company's engine shed was located just to the south of Syke Street bridge, and was a handsome structure of red brick with stone dressings, measuring 117 ft. in length by 70 ft. in width. It was later provided with an eight horsepower steam engine for turning lathes and other items of machinery, on the most approved principle by Mr. Hicks of Bolton.

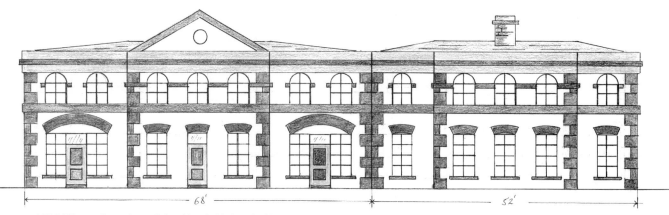

1838 West elevation of the North Union buildings on the Charles Street side of the station. Unfortunately, the rest of the station did not reach the same standards of design. The section on the left was the main entrance and had a full-length canopy. *(Drawing from fragments by author)*

LNWR No 300, 2-2-2 loco under construction. Circa 1852. *(Illustrated London News, December 18, 1852)*

## FOOTNOTES

(1) **Charles Blacker Vignoles, 1793 – 1875.**

In 1814 he gained a commission in the Royal Scots regiment, and after some time in Europe, he returned to England in 1816 where he got married and travelled to America some 12 months later. His original intention was to serve under Simon Bolivar, but instead became assistant state civil engineer in Charleston, South Carolina. He later moved further south and published a map of Florida in 1823. In 1836, he suggested the use of a flat-bottomed rail for use on the London & Croydon Railway. It had been invented by an American, R. L. Stevens, in 1830, but was first manufactured in a British steel works, and became universally known as the Vignoles rail. It was not used widely on standard gauge track until the mid 20th century.

Vignoles carried out a second survey of the Liverpool & Manchester Railway, which was critical of George Stephenson's work, and Joseph Locke carried out an investigative survey of the tunnelling works on the same line, finding several levelling faults in the course of the construction work. Stephenson wasn't pleased with this criticism, but appreciated the skills that these two men possessed, and appointed them as assistant engineers.

(2) The stone blocks varied in size, but were usually around 24 x 24 x 12 inches. Two holes of 1 1/4″ diameter by 6″ deep were bored into the stone and filled with oak plugs, which provided a firm bed for the iron spikes. These blocks were preferred to wooden sleepers, as horses could pull vehicles along without the danger of losing their footing.

(3) The first and sometimes only porter at the station was Thomas Hilton, of Lauderdale Street. He later took up a job as pointsman at Fishergate tunnel, which he held until 1864, when he became pointsman at Strand Road on the Dock Branch. He died on May 26, 1868. (Preston chronicle, May 30, 1868).

# The Lancaster & Preston Junction Railway

Joseph Locke. *(Author's collection)*

Joseph Locke [1] had already looked at the possibility of engineering a line from Preston to Glasgow as early as 1835. His subsequent report on this survey prompted a meeting in the Town Hall at Lancaster, whereupon he was commissioned by a provisional committee of businessmen to carry out a survey for a line from Lancaster to Preston. An Act of Parliament was obtained on May 5, 1837, and work began immediately on the Lancaster & Preston Junction Railway, with an initial capital of £250,000. As with the North Union, the track comprised 65 lb iron rails, laid on transverse timber sleepers on embankments and stone blocks in the cuttings. Locke was appointed consultant engineer, with Mr. A. S. Gee as his assistant.

Construction of the line was carried out in four stages. The first or Lancaster contract extended from the south side of the brook between Lancaster and Scotforth to a peg on the south side of a field, numbered 7 on the plan, in the township of Clevely, the length being 3 miles and 22 chains or thereabouts. The second or Wyre contract extended from the south side of a field numbered 20 on the plan, in the township of Claughton, being in length 5 miles and 21 chains, or thereabouts. The third or Barton contract extended from the south side of that field in Claughton to a peg in a field numbered 7 on the plan, in the township of Preston, the length being 7 miles and 25 chains. The fourth or Preston contract extended to the south of Chatham Street, Preston, being one mile and 3 chains. The work was carried out smoothly and within the estimated time, but well over the engineer's estimated cost, with only one fatality, which occurred on May 29, 1840 at Myerscough, when a 21 ft. section of brickwork on the 35 yard tunnel fell in, while a gang of four men were puddling (waterproofing) the brickwork with clay. Richard Hall, a poor man who lived on Billsborough Lane, died instantly.

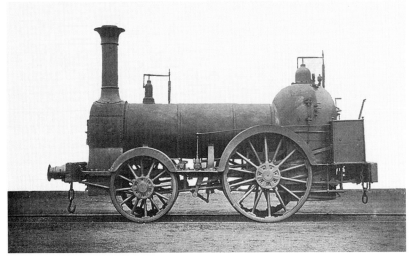

Bury type engine, as used from 1835 to 1844 on the lines around Preston. *(Author's collection)*

The line was officially opened on Thursday, June 25, 1840, and the festive day began when a light engine set off from Preston at 9 o'clock for Lancaster. In the meantime, a large number of people, including local dignitaries and directors from the railway companies, assembled at the North Union station. The crowded train arrived back in Preston just after one o'clock, about half an hour later than expected, and had taken one hour and forty minutes to cover the 20 mile distance, owing to a number of temporary stoppages. Although two tracks had been laid, only one was usable. Shortly after 2 o'clock, the train headed north again with four additional carriages. Enthusiastic crowds lined the route and bridges, waving flags, hats and handkerchiefs. Lancaster was reached in one hour and ten minutes, where the passengers were greeted at Penny Street station by a chorus of 'God save the Queen.' The chairman of the L&PJR, George Burrow, held a banquet for 400 people, with a third comprising elegantly attired ladies in a near-by pavilion. The journey back to Preston commenced at 5 o'clock and took just 55 minutes.

---

**CHEAP AND EXPEDITIOUS TRAVELLING.**

# LANCASTER AND PRESTON JUNCTION RAILWAY.

## A THIRD CLASS CARRIAGE
will be attached to the following trains, viz. :-

From Lancaster to Preston.
7.15 Morning. 10'clock Afternoon.

From Preston to Lancaster.
10.55 Morning. 4.35 Afternoon.

Fares, 1s, 6d, each.

## COACHES
### FROM LANCASTER TO KENDAL,

In connection with the above trains.
Fares:- From Preston to Kendal, and from Kendal to Preston: 4s. Each

Passengers by these Trains may be booked from Lancaster to Liverpool, or Manchester, at 6s. 6d. Each. The other Trains as already advertised.

Preston Chronicle, 16 July, 1840.

---

The North Union had completed a 77 yard tunnel beneath Fishergate in 1840, and had run two tracks through it in the hope of making a connection with the L&P. The construction work cost £20,000, and the L&P contributed £1,500 towards it. The N.U. anticipated them using their station, but they decided to build a terminus on the north side of Fishergate at Dock Street, in the vicinity of the Lancaster Canal. It had originally been the intention of the N.U. to build a line from their station to Dock Street and they approached the L&P with a view to having a joint station there. Once the L&PJR had opened, the inevitable animosity with the N.U. ensued, with heated disputes over the extension and the station at Butler Street. The L&P had previously agreed to pay £300 per annum to run their trains into the N.U. Station, but withdrew their offer when they realised that they had not been obliged (by law) to pay something towards the cost of the tunnel. The situation remained in deadlock for some months until the L&P accepted an offer from the N.U. to supply locomotives at a charge of two shillings and fourpence per train-mile and two shillings and sixpence for double-

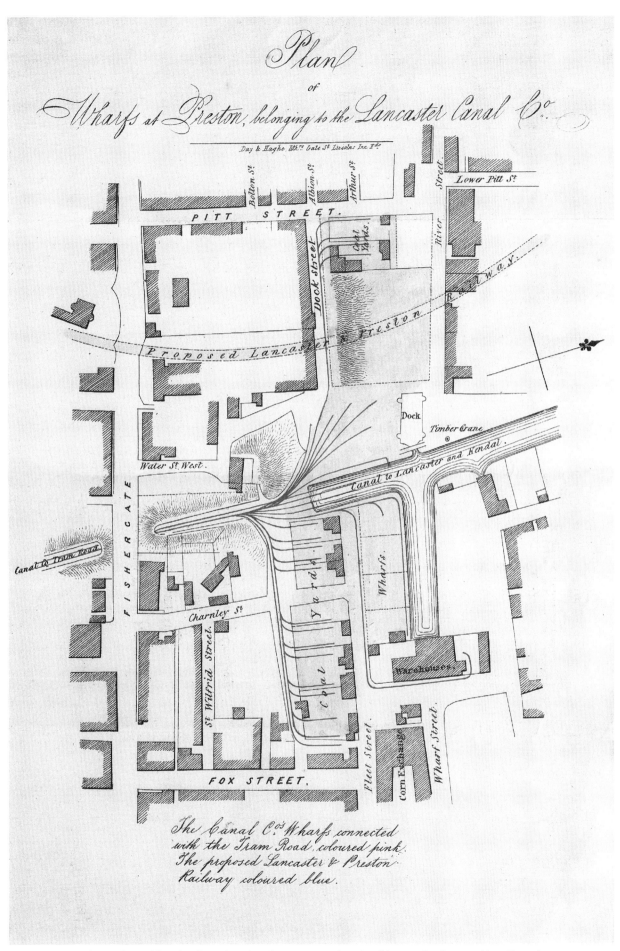

*Plan*

*of*

*Wharfs at Preston, belonging to the Lancaster Canal Co.*

Day & Haghe Lith.rs Gate St Lincolns Inn F.ds

Lower Pitt St.

Bolton St.

Albion St.

Arthur St.

River Street.

PITT STREET.

Coal Yards.

Dock street

Proposed Lancaster & Preston Railway

Dock

Timber Crane

Canal to Lancaster and Kendal.

Water St. West.

Canal to Tram Road

FISHERGATE

Charnley St.

St. Wilfrid Street.

Coal Yards

Wharfs.

Warehouses.

Corn Exchange

Fleet Street.

Wharf Street.

FOX STREET.

*The Canal Co.s Wharfs connected
with the Tram Road coloured pink.
The proposed Lancaster & Preston
Railway coloured blue.*

An early and fascinating plan showing proposed route of Lancaster line, and location of tramroad tunnel, coal yards and canal wharfs. *(Lancashire Records Office)*

heading. This didn't last long, however, as the L&P came under criticism regarding the inferior quality of the track and, what was considered to be, too many unnecessary stoppages.(2) The situation became untenable and the locomotive contract was terminated in December, 1841. The L&P later bought four of the Bury type, four-coupled locomotives, and endeavoured to do business with the Bolton & Preston Railway which, by this time, had got its line as far as Chorley, and was ready to negotiate with the L&P over a joint station and provide them with locomotives. A Preston historian describes how things were at that time: *As showing the weak character of the old engines, we may observe that often, when a heavy train was leaving Preston for the north, porters had to push at the side by way of giving them assistance.*(3) The L&P terminus at Dock Street was little more than a siding with buffer stops and a short, low timber platform. Access to Fishergate was by way of a cinder path and flight of stone steps. Passengers booked to travel further south on the through train had to pay a toll of sixpence, and rather than do this, many of them chose to alight at the terminus, walk across Fishergate, descend the ramp at Butler Street and re-join the train they had just left. The officers of the N.U. tried to put a stop to this practice by flagging the train off before the 'walkers' arrived. A branch line was later taken off the L&P and a small station constructed for the B&P on a site named Maxwell House.

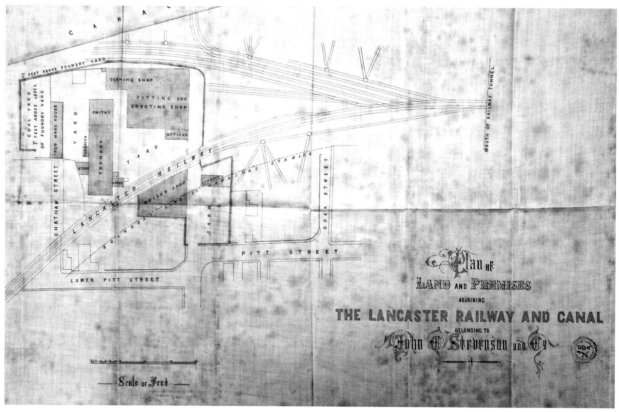

Early plan showing course of Lancaster line in conjuction with Stevenson's Foundry, canal and coal sidings, prior to the replacement of the tunnel with the Fishergate bridge. *(Lancashire Records Office)*

Boundary stone, between N.U. and L&P.R. property, still extant in the 1960's. *(Tony Gillett)*

By 1842, the L&P found itself in severe financial difficulties. Low passenger returns, lack of funds for the much needed upgrading of the permanent way and signalling systems; exorbitantly high fares and the on-going difficulties with the N.U. and Lancaster & Carlisle Railway had placed them in a perilous situation, which was relieved to some extent when the directors agreed to become the lessees of the Lancaster Canal Company on September 1, 1842, for a period of 21 years at £30,000 per annum. Such had been the state of affairs between all concerned, that the L&C.R. arranged for a survey to be carried out by Joseph Locke for an alternative route from Preston to Lancaster. Had it materialised, the line would have been run to the west of the existing one, passing through Garstang and Cockerham. All parties came to their senses following an inspecting officer's report on a fatal accident which occurred at Bay Horse station, on August 21, 1848. The 9 a.m. Euston to Glasgow express which was scheduled to leave Preston at 3. 10 p.m. left at 4. 24 p.m. and, owing to this delay, the 3.45 p.m. local train to Lancaster (operated by the canal company) was permitted to leave Preston at 3. 59 p.m. This train was standing at Bay Horse station, unprotected by the signals when the express ran into the back of it. The inspector cited several factors which had contributed to the accident, the main ones being uncertainty about the ownership of the line; want of co-operation between the L&CR and the lessees of the L&PR, and the want of adequate accommodation at Preston station, which was the cause of delays to north-bound traffic. The L&CR was opened on December 17, 1846, and negotiations resumed in 1848, which ended in an agreement whereby the L&C was to take over the management of the L&P and canal company. This inevitably resulted in the L.C.C. relinquishing its lease of the L&P, which would have had another 14 years to run before its expiry. In November 1848, an application was made for an extension of the line from Dock Street to a junction with the then proposed Preston Extension (East Lancashire Railway Act, 1847), at a point near East Cliff, thus by-passing Fishergate tunnel and the N.U. station. The East Lancashire Railway was in full agreement with this, as they too did not relish the prospect of sharing the N.U. station. The application, however, was rejected by Parliament, much to the disappointment of all concerned. On August 13, 1859, the L.&P. was fully amalgamated with the L.&C. and the L.C.C. became the property of the L.N.W.R. In 1885.

---

# To be sold by Auction
## By Mr. George Parker

On Tuesday, 26th Oct. 1841,
at Twelve O'clock at Noon, at Cadeley Bridge on the
Lancaster and Preston Junction Railway

A LARGE quantity of OLD TIMBER,
in Lots of various Scantlings;
a number of Wheeling PLANKS and BARROWS;
a great variety of OLD IRON;
three good CART HORSES; ten CARTS,
and several Sets of HARNESS complete.
Also 1500 STONE BLOCKS, 2 by 2 by 1.
For particulars apply to the Owner or Auctioneer.

Preston Chronicle, 22 October, 1841.

---

The ordeal of travelling in roofless carriages continued for some time after the line opened. In March 1845, for example, a gentleman booked at Liverpool for Lancaster, paying the whole fare through. The Superintendent at Liverpool was very obliging and directed him to one of the North Union Company's second class carriages, which were similar in design to those of the Liverpool & Manchester.

The carriage was closed up with glazing above the doors and side-lights (side windows), making them every bit as good as the first class except for the lining and cushions. He was quite comfortable and expected to travel the full length of the journey in it. When the train arrived at Preston, however, he and all the other passengers for Lancaster were turned out and transferred to open carriages. The weather at that time was bitterly cold, with strong winds, rain and sleet, which resulted in him catching a severe cold. The superintendent at Preston, Mr. Wilcockson, explained to him that this serious and dangerous annoyance arose form the Lancaster Canal Company's manager obstinately refusing to allow any covered-in second class carriages to run on the L & P. R . He went on to say that barely a day passed where there were no serious complaints about this practice and the delays at the N.U. station, in consequence of all passengers having to be shifted both ways by each train.[4] In 1850, the L&P was approached by the proprietors of the Steam Mill works on Fylde Road, with a view to their premises being served by a siding. Nothing came of this, and the mill was put up for sale in 1854.[5]

## FOOTNOTES

[1] **Joseph Locke 1805 – 1860.**
Began his working life in Yorkshire as a mining engineer, and before getting involved in railway construction, he worked for a time at Stephenson's locomotive works on Forth Street, Newcastle – upon – Tyne. Prior to this he, together with Vignoles, had been assistant to George Stephenson, during the construction of the Liverpool & Manchester Railway. At the time of his survey on a proposed route from Preston to Glasgow, he was chief engineer to the Grand Junction Railway. He will be best remembered for engineering the line from Lancaster to Carlisle,

[2] The rails were made of iron, which tended to shell-off at the tops and sides, leaving an undulating surface. This, together with the fact that they were laid for the most part upon stone blocks, gave the carriages of all classes a rough ride. When steel rails and wooden sleepers were introduced, many of the old limestone blocks were used to construct the base of the tower at Saint Walburg's church.

[3] Hewitson, History of Preston.

[4] Preston Chronicle, March 29, 1845.

[5] Steam Mill contained a 30 h.p. steam engine, five pairs of French stones and two pairs of grey bean-splitters, two flour-dressing machines, a wheat screen and all other requisite machinery for the manufacture of flour and oatmeal. The warehouse had an adjoining drying kiln and was located at the north-west end of L&P's Fylde Road bridge, in close proximity to both the railway and canal. The mill closed many years ago, but the offices are still extant and have been converted to apartments.

# The Bolton & Preston Railway

The company was incorporated by an act of Parliament on July 15, 1837, with the object of connecting Preston with Manchester by way of the Manchester, Bury and Bolton Railway, which was nearing completion at that time.[1] The bill was passed on May 28, 1838 and the line was partly opened from Bolton to Rawlinson's Bridge in 1841. The original plan had been to take the line into Bamber Bridge from Chorley and then use the formation of the Walton Summit tramroad onwards to Preston. A steep gradient and tunnel would have been required on the north bank of the Ribble, and it was the cost of this that led to the abandonment of the idea. It was then decided to make a junction at Euxton and run two independent lines alongside those of the N.U. This was found to be unnecessary, as the N.U. agreed to allow them to use their tracks at the rate of one shilling per passenger.

The line was surveyed by John Urpeth Rastrick, and the man who engineered it was Alexander James Adie. Work commenced in February, 1841 and problems occurred during the construction of a 350 yard tunnel at Hartwood Green near Chorley, where hard clay was encountered and a huge quantity of water had to be pumped out of the ground by seven steam engines. After struggling against the odds for 18 months, it was decided to excavate a cutting instead. The work involved the removal of 650,000 cubic yards of earth and the construction of a road bridge. High, battered stone retaining walls, 3 ft. thick, were required to keep the steep embankment in check, and these were strengthened by a row of 16 flying shores on perpendicular piers, 16 ½ ft. apart, each having an elliptical span of 25 ft. and a rise of 1 ½ ft. at the centre. They comprised single, rock-faced stone voussoirs bearing coursed stonework with flagstone coping in the centres. A short tunnel had to be made at the Euxton end, along with another cutting, 70 ft. in depth with a smaller retaining wall.

While all this work was going on, a temporary terminus was opened on June 15, 1841 at Rawlinson's

Un-rebuilt Scot, 6149 The Middlesex Regiment, piloted by class 2, 4-4-0, 489, at Euxton, Balshaw Lane on July 7, 1938. (*W.D. Cooper*)

Bridge near Adlington, on the Leeds & Liverpool Canal. Horse-drawn coaches went from the Bull & Royal and Red Lion hotels in Preston to meet the trains at Rawlinson's Bridge. There were three trains a day here in each direction. The northbound left Bolton at 8 30 a.m., 3 p.m. and 6 30 p.m., with connecting coaches leaving Rawlinson Bridge at 9 a.m., 3 30 p.m. and 7 p.m. For southbound travellers, coaches left the above hotels in Preston at 7 30 a.m., 2 p.m. and 5 30 p.m. There was usually just one engine in steam and no Sunday services, and the the fares from Bolton to Preston in 1841 were 5s. inside and 3s 6d. outside. Back in 1838, John Wilkinson made arrangements with the M. B. & B. R. to run his coaches from Preston to Manchester via Chorley and the railway station at Bolton. There were just two coaches to begin with, the 'Duke of Manchester' and the 'Doctor'; the former left the mail coach office in Preston every morning at 7 o'clock and arrived in Manchester at 10 o'clock, via New Bailey Street station, Salford. The latter coach left Preston every afternoon except Sunday at 4 o'clock and arrived in Manchester at 7 30, travelling by way of Blackburn and Bolton. In June 1838, he added some new coaches to his fleet, with one or two bearing names pertaining to the new transport technology. The 'Engineer' met the London mail train at 8 30 a.m. and took passengers to Edinburgh via Carlisle and Moffat; the 'Locomotive,' which left for Carlisle at 7 o'clock, where a connection was made with the train to Newcastle; the 'Fylde Union,' which left at 3 30 p.m. for Blackpool via Kirkham and Poulton, and the 'Blackburn Market,' which left Preston every Wednesday at 9 o'clock.

---

# Bolton & Preston Railway.

### TENDERS FOR THE SUPPLY OF LOCOMOTIVE POWER, CARRIAGES AND WAGGONS.

The Directors are prepared to receive Tenders for the Supply of **LOCOMOTIVE POWER, CARRIAGES** and **WAGGONS** upon this line, which is expected to be Opened throughout about the end of April next.

### TENDERS FOR MERCHANDIZE TRAFFIC.

The Directors are also prepared to receive proposals from Carries or others, who may be disposed to enter into arrangements with the Company in regard to the Goods Traffic upon the Line.

Conditions and particulars may be known upon application to the **COMPANY'S SECRETARY, at BOLTON.**

The Directors will meet at the **COMPANY'S OFFICE,** in Bolton, at 11 o'clock, on **THURSDAY,** the 9th day of March next, to consider such tenders as may then be submitted.

By Order,                                                                        PETER SINCLAIR
Bolton, 10th Feb., 1843                                                          Secretary.

*Preston Chronicle, February 1843.*

---

The section from Rawlinson's Bridge to Chorley was opened on December 23, 1841, and although the formation was designed for double track, only a single line existed at the time of opening, as the directors had decided not to have it doubled until the section from Chorley to Euxton had been completed. The junction with the N.U. at Euxton was opened on June 22, 1843 and doubling of the track began shortly after. The station at Rawlinson's Bridge was subsequently closed and replaced by a station at Adlington, and a junction built on the site for a branch to Ellerbeck Colliery. The station at Maxwell House on the north side of Fishergate in Preston was never used by the B&P, as an agreement had been reached with the N.U. to use their station and facilities at Butler Street. The B&P was still obliged to maintain the old tramroad for which it had no further use, paying the LCC an annual sum in excess of £ 7,000. This continued until the company was absorbed into the N.U. on May 10, 1844. The Blackburn & Preston Railway was opened in 1846, accessing Preston by way of a junction with the N.U. at Farington. There followed 4 years of confusion, congestion and bitter arguments between all concerned, until the Preston Extension was completed in 1850.(2)

Competition with the N.U. for the Manchester traffic hotted up within weeks of the opening in 1843, and the situation, as was the case with so many other railway companies at that time, became acrimonious. Although the N.U. tried to put a spoke in the wheel by deliberately detaining Manchester-bound trains at Preston for up to half an hour at a time, and running their own special trains to Manchester, the B&P continued to carry an average of 1,800 passengers a week at a toll of one shilling for each passenger. To overcome the delays, they returned to carrying passengers from Preston to Euxton by road, and approached the LCC with a view to moving coal trains along the tramroad. Notwithstanding the perverse tactics of the N.U., it was still quicker to get to Manchester by way of Euxton and Bolton than using the route to Parkside and the L&M. The situation was resolved and fares were reduced considerably following the inevitable amalgamation of the N.U. and B&P.R.

## FOOTNOTES

(1) The Manchester, Bury & Bolton Railway was formed by the proprietors of the Manchester, Bolton & Bury Canal and Navigation Company in 1831. The 10 mile route from Salford to Bolton was to have been constructed for the most part upon the line of the canal, but was eventually run alongside it. The biggest contract was for a 295 yard tunnel near Farnworth, which had double portals of different sizes. The line from Salford Central to Bolton Trinity Street opened in 1838.

(2) For more details see The Lancashire & Yorkshire Railway around Preston, by the same author.

# Preston & Wyre Railway

The original P&W terminus at Maudland showing the crossing, engine shed and goods station *(Harris Library)*

The Preston & Wyre Railway & Dock Company was the result of a merger in 1839 of the Preston & Wyre Railway & Harbour Company (formed in 1835) and the Preston & Wyre Dock Company (formed in 1837). Peter Hesketh Fleetwood was the driving force behind the project and provided much of the funding.(1) He appointed George Thomas Landmann, a former army officer and military engineer, who was at that time civil engineer to the London & Greenwich Railway, to carry out a survey for a line from the Maudland area in Preston to the site of a proposed dock on the Wyre estuary in 1835. At the same time, the London architect, Decimus Burton, was drawing up plans for a new town, which was later named Fleetwood after its founder; and perhaps the most splendid and prominent of his creations for the new port were the Pharos and Beach lighthouses (1840) and the North Euston Hotel (1841).[2] The route of the railway was considered to be quite favourable for all concerned, as the entire 17 ½ mile length could be made without interfering with any parks, ornamental or villa grounds, and without touching more than one very inferior building. The total difference in levelling was found to be 41 ft., the highest point or summit being the terminus at Preston, which was approximately 600 ft. distant from the then terminus of the N.U. station. The greatest inclination of the line did not exceed 7 ft. 6 ins. per mile in a 4 mile section, the whole of the remainder being almost level.

The quantity of earth removed for cuttings equalled the amount required for embankments, and the clay was found to be favourable for the manufacture of bricks, which saved a considerable amount of expense. At the Preston end, a brick viaduct of about 600 ft. in length with a height of 25 ft. carried the railway across a narrow and abrupt valley. The viaduct was ornamented with dressed stonework until it was widened on both sides to take four tracks by the Lancashire & Yorkshire Railway in 1885. Evidence of the widening is plainly visible today, as the extension work was done using blue Staffordshire bricks. It was also found that the River Wyre was free from any intricacies, its channel from the sea being four or five miles in length and 200 yards wide. From half flood to half ebb, vessels drawing 16 ft. of water could enter safely; and at high water, during spring tides, the channel had 36 ft. of water and had never less than 5 ft. The anchorage throughout the channel was found to be on good holding ground.

The following is Landmann's estimate for the construction of the line for a single road, but including the cost of land, bridges and viaducts for a double line:-

| Item: | £ |
|---|---|
| Land | 17,500 |
| Cuttings & embankments | 25,500 |
| Draining & Fencing | 4,000 |
| Bridges | 3,000 |
| Viaduct near Preston | 6,000 |
| Stone blocks & sleepers | 5,148 |
| Rails, chairs &c. and laying | 18,862 |
| Turn plates &c. | 500 |
| Ballasting | 4,500 |
| Gates & lodges | 1,000 |
| Embankment in the Wyre | 4,500 |
| Wharf & warehouses | 11,000 |
| Engines & carriages | 8,000 |
|  | 109,000 |
| Add for contingencies, rather more than 1/10th | 10,900 |
|  | 120,000 |

Access to the station at Maudland [3] was by way of a crossing on the level with the L&P, whose tracks were 5 ft. higher at that point. The P&W was, therefore, obliged to raise the level of its tracks accordingly. At the same time, a connection was made with the L&P so that Fleetwood trains could run into the N.U. station. An omnibus service operated between Maudland and Butler Street for connections with the N.U. at 6d. per traveller. The Maudland crossing was a potentially dangerous place, especially when it was operated under the primitive system of the day. The first accident took place on December 18, 1840, when a stationary ballast train on the L&P was hit by a train coming from the Fleetwood direction, resulting in the death of the ballast operator. The subsequent enquiry revealed that the man in charge of the crossing, or 'Policeman' as such people were referred to, was unable to show a red light to the P&W train, as his hand lamp had been sent off to Lancaster for repair, and that his warning to the ballast operator had been wilfully ignored. It was also noted that the P&W engine was not carrying any lights, and that there were no written rules and regulations available to the policeman

# PRESTON AND WYRE RAILWAY AND HARBOUR COMPANY.

## Iron Rails, Chairs, &c.

# TO IRON MASTERS.

The Directors of the PRESTON and WYRE RAILWAY and HARBOUR COMPANY are ready to receive TENDERS for the supply of about 70,000 Lineal Yards of Parallel Malleable IRON RAILS, of the weight of 50lbs. Per yard; and also for 70,000 Cast Iron Chairs, of the weight of 18lbs. Each, with the necessary quantity of the Pins and keys. For further particulars apply to GEORGE LANDMANN, ESQUIRE, the Company's Engineer, No. 4 King William Street, London Bridge. Tenders to be delivered, Signed and Sealed, and addressed to the Directors of the Preston and Wyre Railway and Harbour Company, on or before the 1st day of January, 1836.

By Order,
    OWEN T. ALGER, Secretary.

15th Dec. 1835. No. 26, Cornhill, London.

*Preston Chronicle, 19 December, 1835.*

regarding procedure at such crossings. The second serious accident occurred on Sunday, September 18, 1845, when an excursion train bound for Fleetwood with some 30 open carriages was cut in two at the crossing by a delayed up train from Lancaster, which was travelling around 30 mph, instead of the regulatory 10mph for the approach to the crossing. There were many injuries but, amazingly, no fatalities. The construction of a third track across the L&P, just to the north of the existing crossing in 1850, only added to the risk of further accidents. This was part of the ill-fated Fleetwood, Preston & West Riding Junction Railway, which was intended to run from Deepdale to Maudland and connect with the P&W on the west side of the crossing. For a more detailed account, see the Preston & Longridge chapter. The P&W layout at Maudland comprised a small station, single track engine shed and a goods shed served by two tracks.

The cost of the Tulketh viaduct (later to become known as Maudland viaduct) escalated to over twice the estimate, at £14,000, and work was set back for some time following a tragic accident on February 22, 1840, when one of the arches collapsed killing 11 workmen. The line was ceremoniously opened on Wednesday, July 15, 1840, with the first train leaving Preston at 11.45. The locomotives 'Duchess' and 'North Star' double-headed a train of 11 carriages and the 19 ¾ mile journey was completed satisfactorily in just under an hour. Thousands of people turned out to witness the event and there was much jubilation, with naval guns being fired at Fleetwood. George Landmann wasn't there on that occasion, as he had been replaced by George and Robert Stephenson some time before the construction work was completed. Normal traffic workings commenced the following day, with North Union locomotives having been contracted to work the line. Trains left Preston for Fleetwood at 7 40 a.m., 12 40 p.m. and 5.30 p.m. The Fleetwood to Preston trains ran at 8 5 a.m., 12 40 p.m. and 4 45 p.m. By 1845, the company had six locomotives, 23 carriages and 86 wagons of its own on the books.

The fares were:

|  | 1st Class | 2nd Class | 3rd Class |
|---|---|---|---|
| Preston to Fleetwood | 4s. | 5s. | 2s. |
| Preston to Poulton | 3s. | 2s. 3d. | 1s. 6d. |
| Preston to Kirkham | 1s. 9d. | 1s. 3d. | 9d. |

The above fares were applicable to Maudland station only, and passengers travelling from the North Union station had to pay an extra sixpence. The steamer, 'Express' was scheduled to leave Fleetwood for Ulverston via Bardsea shortly after the arrival of the first train from Preston, and to return in time for the last train of the day back. The price of a cabin was 4 shillings and the deck, 2 shillings; carriages one pound and horses ten shillings each. The laying of a second track began in February, 1845. There were steam packet offices at Fleetwood and Ulverston, and the following year saw an expansion in the steamer services, with the company's ship, 'Fire King' sailing to Ardrossen; the 'Benledi' to Douglas, Isle of Man; the 'Victoria' to Belfast, and the 'Prince Albert' to Dumfries via Whitehaven. In 1843, the steamer, 'Nile' was sailing from Fleetwood to Piel Island, with excursions to the castle and Furness Abbey. This steamer also sailed from the old quay at Marsh End, Preston for Fleetwood, with passengers returning the same day by train. In 1845, the steamers, 'Her Majesty' and 'Royal Consort' ran trips to Glasgow from Fleetwood. Mr. W, Parker, proprietor of the Sun Hotel, which was the commercial and posting house in Ulverston, had post chaises, gigs and coaches available for the conveyance of passengers from the Fleetwood packets to all parts of the Lake District. He was also proprietor of the refreshment rooms at Furness Abbey station, and ran an omnibus service between Ulverston and the railway station at Dalton. The steamer services from Fleetwood declined rapidly once the railway routes to Barrow, Carlisle and Scotland had been established.

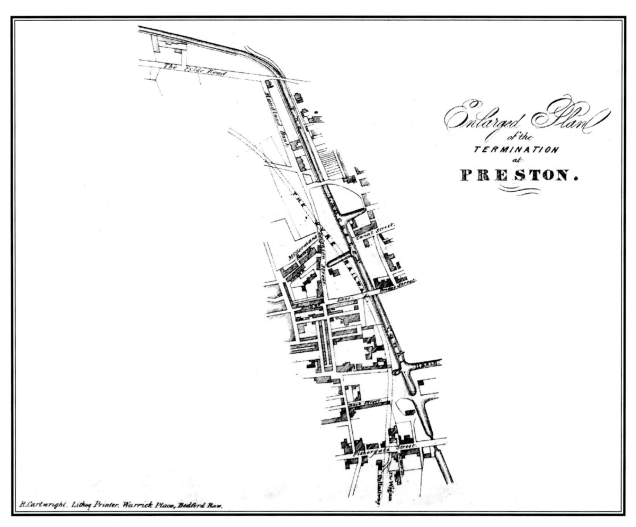

Plan showing the proposed route of the P&W.R. at the Preston end. *(Lancashire Records Office)*

Within 12 months of the opening, goods such as corn, meal, potatoes and other similar produce were arriving at Fleetwood harbour from all parts of the country and conveyed by the railway to Preston at the rate of two shillings per ton. Other charges included, on the vessel, 3d. per ton per annum; or 1d. per ton for the Walney light; 3d. per ton per annum or 1d. per ton each voyage until the 3d. per annum was paid for the three lights at Fleetwood, and 1d. per ton for harbour dues, and on goods; 6d. per ton for wharfage. The goods were craned out of the vessels and into the railway wagons without lightering or carting. The tonnage rate for heavier items included pig iron, 2s.; bar iron, 3s.; ale and porter in casks, 2s. 6d.; timber, 3s.; cotton, hemp, flax and bale goods, 4s. 6d.; wine and spirits in casks, 7s.; coal for export, 1s. 6d.; cattle, sheep or pigs, 10s. per wagon. There were no charges for wharfage and the use of cranes, so long as the goods were being transferred from the docks by railway to Poulton, Kirkham, Preston and beyond. The original 1840 terminus at Fleetwood was on Dock Street, and lasted until 1883, when it was replaced by a larger and much more impressive station on Queen's Terrace, which was closed to all traffic in 1966 and subsequently demolished, following the Beeching recommendations. From then on, trains terminated at Wyre Dock station at the south end of Dock Street.

Rebuilt Scot, 46156, The South Wales Borderer, with a fast train to the Fylde at Cottam, on April 29, 1962. *(Tony Gillett)*

A single track branch line from Kirkham to Lytham, called the Lytham & Preston Branch Railway, was opened on February 17, 1846. No major obstacles were encountered on the line of construction, and the total cost amounted to £30.000. A small dock was also built on the banks of the Ribble at Lodge Road, Lytham. Fares from Preston to Lytham: 3rd class, 1s. 6d.; 2nd class, 2s. 6d. and 1st class, 3s. 6d. Prior to the construction of the Lytham branch, on or after Sunday, June 3, 1843, passengers travelled from Maudland station to Kirkham and then on to Lytham by omnibus. The fares for first class railway and inside omnibus were 3s. 0d.; second class, 2s. 0d., and third class, outside omnibus, 1s. 6d. Later on that year, a 3 ¾ mile branch from Poulton to Blackpool (Talbot Road)was opened together with a short branch to Lytham Dock.

With the commencement of construction work on the Lancaster & Carlisle Railway, a meeting was held at the Crown Hotel, Fleetwood on September 10, 1845, to discuss the feasibility of extending the P&W line north of Fleetwood, crossing the Wyre and joining up with the L&C just to the south of the River Lune, via Pilling and Cockerham, following the course of the future Glasson Dock branch (which was not built until 1883). Although railway-mania was all the rage at the time, the idea was shelved indefinitely. A new station was opened at Thornton on April 1, 1865.

On July 28, 1849, the P&W was vested jointly between the LNWR (one third) and the LYR (two thirds). It was then referred to as the Preston & Wyre Joint Railway. Some nine months later, on April 13, 1850, what must have been the longest trip ever made by an unmanned locomotive took place at Fleetwood. Shortly after the arrival of a luggage train, the engine was left in the charge of a person who had the job of turning, watering and stoking up in preparation for the return journey. The regulator must have been left or knocked open, for as the steam pressure increased, the engine started moving of its own

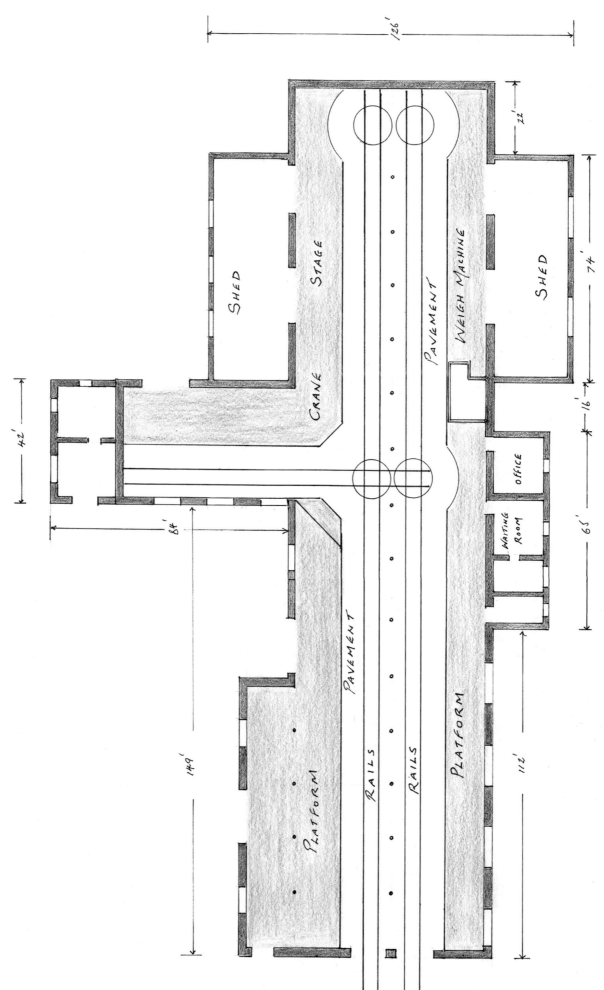

Prteston & Wyre Goods shed plan. (Author)

accord, and the man, unable to comprehend the situation, tried turning different levers, including the whistle valve, then panicked and jumped off the footplate. The engine began to gather speed in the direction of Preston, with the steam-whistle giving fair warning to station masters and gate keepers on the line of its approach. The crew of a passenger train at Fleetwood, on seeing the incident, quickly uncoupled the engine and set off in pursuit of the runaway. Unfortunately the fire was low and there wasn't enough steam pressure to provide the power needed to catch up. The runaway reached Preston in 20 minutes at a rate of about a mile a minute, and on its arrival it ran into a rake of empty coal wagons belonging to a local coal merchant named Pearson, which had been placed on the up line from Fleetwood, as no arrivals from there were expected at that time. Thankfully, this blockade of wagons prevented the engine from passing through the tunnel to the passenger station, where its arrival might have been met with disastrous consequences. Most of the wagons were shivered to pieces and the front of the engine was staved in, with a loss to the Lancashire & Yorkshire Railway of £300. By some miracle no lives were lost and no individual injured.[4]

Joint railway cap badge for P&WR section. *(Courtesy, Paul Atherton)*

Prior to the arrival of the railways north of Parkside, a group of Preston businessmen had got together with a view to obtaining an act to build what would have been the Preston and Lytham Ship Canal. The Ribble was deemed to be unreliable for the purpose of conveying goods to a port in Preston, as most of the vessels had to wait for spring tides before they could safely navigate up river; any vessel arriving at Lytham during the course of neap tides would have to unload at that point and have all goods taken to Preston by carts. A rough survey was carried out in August 1834, which allowed for a canal depth of 14 ft. 6 ins., capable of taking a vessel of 250 tons; a connecting pool at Lytham and a basin at Preston, including bridges, culverts and an aqueduct at Freckleton at £105,000. Had it gone ahead, the final figure would have been well over twice that of the estimate.

## FOOTNOTES

[1] Peter Hesketh Fleetwood 1801 – 1866. Born Peter Hesketh at Wennington Hall, near Lancaster, and later added the Fleetwood after one of his ancestors. He became an MP and was later created a Baronet. Following his education at Oxford, where he met and befriended the architect Decimus Burton, he moved to a family estate on the North Lancashire coast. He was enthusiastic about the development of the railways, and devoted much of his time and money in bringing the railway to the Fylde coast. Notwithstanding the success of the railway and docks, and the development of Fleetwood as a port, he had to sell his estate at Rossall Hall and move back to London.

[2] Decimus Burton 1800 – 1881. The unusual first name was awarded him by virtue of the fact that he was the tenth child of the family. He studied at Oxford and became an architect, specialising in the setting out of large ornamental gardens. He will be best remembered for planning the layout at Hyde Park and the Royal Botanic Gardens at Kew.

[3] The original plan was for the line to run parallel with Maudland Bank and the canal, at the east end of Dock Street, and then join the North Union at Fishergate. The line would have followed the same route as the coal sidings from Bridge Lane.

[4] Preston Chronicle, April 18, 1850.

# Preston & Longridge Railway

The Preston & Longridge Railway Company was incorporated by an Act of Parliament on July 14, 1836, and opened for traffic on May 1, 1840. The 6 ½ mile line was built mainly for the purpose of transporting stone from the quarries at Tootal Heights, Longridge to the terminus at Deepdale Street in Preston. The good quality stone was in much demand for buildings in Preston, and later on it was used in the construction of railway bridges, churches, public buildings, wharves and the new docks. It was also used for the manufacture of setts, flag stones, kerbs and drainage culverts for Preston Corporation. Large quantities of stone had already been hauled to Preston by cart for the construction of the N.U. infrastructure, and shipped to Liverpool for the construction of new docks. Quarry owner, Thomas Fleming, and local entrepreneur, Peter Hesketh Fleetwood put forward the idea for a railway in 1835, using the premise that where 'two horses on the road would struggle to draw three tons of stone per day, they would be able to pull 40 tons with less effort on a railway.' The 5 ¾ mile single line section from Longridge station to Deepdale Street had an intermediate station at Grimsargh and was initially worked by horses.

In 1846, an enterprising company calling itself the Fleetwood, Preston and West Riding Joint Railway, applied for powers to build a 16 mile line from the P&W near Maudland to a junction at Deepdale on the P&L, about a quarter of a mile from the Preston terminus, then on to Grimsargh where it was to branch off towards the Ribble valley and traverse the north bank to Clitheroe by way of Mitton, and form a junction with the Blackburn, Clitheroe and North Western Railway. Another junction was planned for a line to Elslack near Skipton on the Leeds & Bradford Extension Railway; there were also plans to build a branch to Burnley and lease the P&L. The company was incorporated on July 12, 1846, and took over the P&L on January 1, 1847, at an annual rent of £3,000 ; in the meantime, tenders had been invited for the construction of the section from Longridge to Clitheroe and the 1 ½ mile Maudland extension. The latter was the only part of the route ever to be completed, and involved the construction of 5 over-bridges, an iron bridge crossing the Lancaster canal and a double-track tunnel with open cuttings, 862 yards long, which was locally referred to as 'Miley Tunnel.' The line joined the P&L at what was to become Deepdale Junction and was opened on January 14, 1850. Steam traction took over from the horses in 1848, and on June 12 that year a locomotive bearing the name 'Addison' (after the company's chairman), hauled a special train carrying 150 guests and directors the full length of the line. The train had to be divided at the foot of the steep climb into Longridge, as the engine had only enough power to drag half of it up at a time.

Miley Tunnel, looking towards Deepdale. *(Tony Gillett)*

Map showing Deepdale backshunt. *(Harris Library)*

The F. P & W. R. J. R. sold off the old Lancaster & Preston railway stock in September 1849, and replaced it with 2 locomotives, 8 roofed carriages, 8 open carriages and 7 goods wagons. Following a period of financial shortcomings and the subsequent closure of the line for a period of three weeks in 1852, the PLR stepped in and resumed ownership. This, however, was only to last for four years, when, on June 23, 1856, the F.P. & W.R.J.R. obtained powers to purchase the PLR as from September 1st that year. The price was £48,000, made payable in eight instalments at two-yearly intervals. A new station, called Maudland Bridge, was built between the canal bridge and tunnel, comprising timber platforms and a small hut, from which tickets were issued. Other stations added to the line included, Deepdale Bridge (1850), replacing the terminus building on Deepdale Street, which continued to serve as a coal and goods yard (the name being changed to Deepdale in 1867); Gamull lane (1854), which was south of Grimsargh and referred to by locals as 'Gammer Lane;' the name was changed to Fulwood two years later and, in order to effectively confuse all in sundry, the name was changed again to Ribbleton on October 1, 1900. A small halt, also bearing the name Ribbleton, was erected in 1863. It comprised a single stone platform and was intended for use by soldiers and their families at the near-by Fulwood Barracks. It saw very little use and was closed some 5 years later.

Deepdale Mill Street crossing, with crossing-keeper's cottage on the left. *(British Railways)*

The keeper's cottage was rented out by B.R. In the 1960's. It is seen here in tidy condition with curtains etc.
The track in the foreground was the only one in use. *(British Railways)*

A fireman's view of Deepdale Junction from the footplate of a 'Big Eight' in the early 1960's.
The locomotive has just passed through Deepdale Mill Street crossing. *(Tony Gillett)*

A further application for the extension of the line from Grimsargh to Clitheroe and a connection with the Midland Railway at Elslack was made by the F.P.&W.R.J.R. in 1866, but it was strongly and effectively opposed by the mighty London & North Western and Lancashire & Yorkshire Railway Companies. The F.P.&W.R.J.R shareholders accepted a generous offer and the company withdrew the bill; the inevitable outcome being that on June 17, 1867, the line came under the joint ownership of the L.&N.W. and L&Y companies. This arrangement didn't go down well with the factory owners and merchants of Preston, as it was well known at that time that the new proprietors of the Longridge Branch had agreed to share the traffic and that no competition existed between them. The Arrival of the Midland Railway via Grimsargh would have brought about much needed competition and all companies serving the town would have been obliged to review their goods rates accordingly. On June 25, 1892, a meeting was held at the Co-operative Hall in Longridge for yet another fruitless extension. This time it was a proposal to extend the line to Slaidburn via Chipping and Newton, making a connection with Little North Western line to Ingleton.

An early photo of the keeper's cottage
with a 5-lever L.N.W. ground frame,
and a 'Bobby' of a different kind
on the right. *(Courtesy, Paul Gregson)*

Signalman, Tommy Balshaw
proudly poses outside his
box at Deepdale Junction.
*(Courtesy, Paul Gregson)*

Following the opening of the Maudland – Deepdale extension in 1850, it had been possible to move goods only from Longridge to the N.U. station at Preston, by way of the P&W and L&P sections, albeit with some tricky and often precarious shunting manoeuvres. A connecting curve was put in between Maudland Bridge and a point just to the north of the No 5 signal box, and opened for passengers and goods on June 1, 1885. The bridge-work was carried out by McGregor's of Southport, who widened the existing iron railway bridge and built an impressive new brick bridge with semicircular arch to take Maudland Road over the canal. The station at Maudland Bridge was subsequently closed amid protests from local people.[1] In 1888, a privately owned single track railway was built to serve a large mental hospital at Whittingham. A small terminus was erected at Grimsargh, with a connection to the Longridge railway. The line carried passengers (mainly hospital staff and visitors) and goods which comprised for the most part, coal for the boilers, and general medical equipment. There was no signalling system as such, and throughout its life-span of 69 years, an odd assortment of steam

Courtaulds exchange sidings in September 1965, with the crew of Pecket 0-4-0 saddle tank, 2086, taking a breather. I hope they remembered to put something on the cold steel rail before sitting on it! *(Tony Gillett)*

Preston guard, Bob Scott, is ready for action with his hickory shunting pole, as he sets the points for the Banana Sidings. *(Tony Gillett)*

locomotives and rolling stock was used to provide a daily shuttle service. In the final years leading up to its complete closure in 1957, the passengers were carried back and forth in converted ex - L.N.W. 4-wheeled brake vans. Most of the engines were four-coupled saddle and side tanks, but in 1947, the management took delivery of an ex-Southern Railway Stroudley class D1, 0-4-2 tank locomotive, which carried the name, James Friars, after the Hospital chairman. The last engine to work on the line was a Sentinel 0-4-0 industrial tank, named 'Gradwell,' which had formerly worked at Bolton Corporation gas works. She looked more like a Diesel shunter than a steamer, and presented an odd but fascinating sight with a train of green-coloured brake vans behind her.

The P&L.R never made much on the passenger service trains, which had been improved somewhat over the years, but it was all too late. By 1930, the roads in the area had been upgraded and competitive bus services were making a big impact on the shorter railway routes in North Lancashire. The P&L.R. came under the ownership of the London, Midland and Scottish Railway in 1923, and in accordance with their rationalisation programme, it was closed to passenger traffic on June 2, 1930. Passenger services were also withdrawn from the neighbouring Garstang & Knott End and Glasson Dock branches in the same year. At around this time, the quarry business at Longridge was diminishing, leaving coal and coke as the main cargoes carried north of Deepdale. All was not lost, however, when a large viscose factory was opened at Redscar by Courtaulds Ltd. in 1938. A branch was taken off the line north of Ribbleton and exchange sidings constructed for the delivery of coal and other commodities. The factory had its own four-coupled saddle tanks for shunting, which were replaced by a Sentinel Diesel shunter in 1967. In that same year, the section from the Courtaulds branch to Longridge was closed down altogether. The section from Deepdale to the exchange sidings at Redscar was abandoned following the closure of Courtaulds in 1980, and the section from Maudland to Deepdale was closed in 1994, following the withdrawal of coal facilities there.

A view of the long-closed Grimsargh Station and crossing gates in 1965.
The Whittingham branch had been closed for some years at the time this photo was taken, but the terminus building with single-pitch roof was still standing. *(Tony Gillett)*

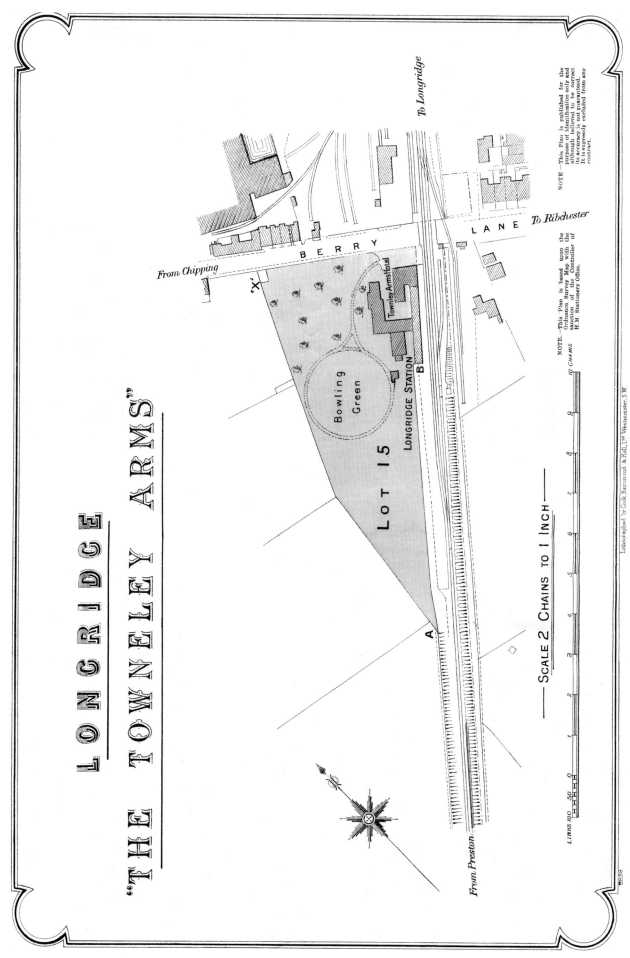

LONGRIDGE

"THE TOWNELEY ARMS"

Lot 15

Bowling Green

Townley Arms Hotel

LONGRIDGE STATION

BERRY LANE

From Chipping

To Longridge

To Ribchester

From Preston

'X'

A

B

— SCALE 2 CHAINS TO 1 INCH —

LINKS 100    50    0                    10 CHAINS    1    2    3    4    5    6    7    8    9

NOTE.—This Plan is based upon the Ordnance Survey Map with the sanction of the Controller of H.M. Stationery Office.

NOTE.—This Plan is published for the purpose of identification only and although believed to be correct its accuracy is not guaranteed. It is expressly excluded from any contract.

Lithographed by Cook, Hammond & Kell, 1 st Westminster, S.W.

L.M.S. Property Dept. plan for the Townley Arms, Longridge in 1935. *(Author's collection)*

42

The skeletal remains of the terminus at Whittingham in September 1969. *(Tony Gillett).*

The impressive portal of the quarry tunnel at Longridge. The arch is of the pointed horseshoe style, with rusticated voussoirs and large keystone. The masonry projection tapers upwards in the style of a pylon, adding strength to the structure. It's fascinating to think how many thousands of tons of stone have passed through this small opening, and on to Preston, where so much of it was fashioned into ashlars by craftsmen for the construction of the town's finest buildings. *(Author)*

A bleak and funereal aspect of the station buildings and crossing at Longridge, on the occasion of a R.C.T.S. rail-tour on September 22, 1962. The tender of Super D loco, 49451, is just visible beyond the gates.
*(G. Harrop)*

## Coal and stone merchants at Deepdale yard

Thomas Langtree, Martin & Maymon, Woods, Banks & Co.

James Dobson & Co., Coal & Slate merchants (late John Rawcliffe), Deepdale Street, Preston. Sole agents for Preston to the Brinsop Hall Coal Co., Best Arley, Orrell, King, Pemberton Yard, Gas coals & slack for house and steam purposes. A large quantity of Welsh slate was always on hand, and the premises incorporated an excellent shoeing forge and jobbing smithy. (1877).

John Rawcliffe Jnr. Coal merchant. (1873).

Cooper & Tullis, quarry owners, building contractors & stone merchants. (1848)

Thomas Banks, Deepdale yard and Longridge station. (1870). Still in business at time of writing.

### FOOTNOTES

(1) Regular meetings of the inhabitants of Maudland and Saint Peter's wards took place at the house of Mrs. Noble, proprietress of the Bridge Inn at Maudland, where issues relating to the future of the station were discussed. The engine of the first train to use the new curve left Preston bedecked with blossoms and heather, and as the train approached the new junction on its return journey, it exploded a number of fog signals in a loud salutation to the long overdue connection.

# CHAPTER TWO

# Lancaster Canal & Dock Street

Aerial photo showing Dock Street area after the canal had been partially drained. *(British Railways Board)*

The first act relating to the Lancaster Canal Company was passed in 1792, and the first section of the work was a 13 ½ mile cut from Kirkless near Wigan to Walton Summit, which opened in 1793. The next section was from Preston to the locks at Tewitfield, a distance of 42 miles; and the section from Tewitfield to Kendal was completed in 1819. The next work, which was sanctioned by an act of 1793, was a three mile branch from Galgate to Glasson Dock, which was opened in 1826. Another act of 1816, sanctioned the construction of a junction with the Leeds & Liverpool Canal at Johnson's Hillock, which was completed in 1819. The whole length of the canal, including the connecting tramroad from Walton Summit to Preston, was 79 miles. John Rennie surveyed the main route from Kirkless to Kendal, and drew up plans for the cuttings, wharves, aqueducts and bridges. Perhaps the work he will be best remembered for is the stately 5 arched aqueduct over the River Lune, which cost the company over £30,000 (2 ½ times the original estimate), leaving little or nothing over with which to build another aqueduct over the Ribble. It was the shortage of funds that led to the construction of a tramway, which fell into disuse once all the railway companies in the area were in operation. The driving force behind the project was Samuel Gregson, and the route of the tramway was surveyed and planned by the Lancaster Canal Company's chief engineer, William Cartwright. The permanent way of what was intended to be a temporary way comprised double track with angled iron rails laid upon stone blocks. The gauge was given as 4 ft. 3 ins. on the final drawings, but this was changed just prior to the commencement of construction to 4 ft. 1 ins., with a space of 3 ft. 8 ins. between the roads. The line was completed in 1803, and ran from the basin at Preston to Walton Summit via Todd

Lane and Bamber Bridge, with steam-powered inclines at Avenham, Penwortham and Walton Summit. Teams of horses were used to haul an average of four large trucks, each having a maximum load of 2 tons, or an average of six of the smaller types. The trucks were quite sturdy and were made of wood, with wrought-iron bracing, trimmings and wheels; some of which were equipped with crude, lever-operated wooden brakes. Relay stables with water and fodder for the horses were erected at certain points along the way.

Canal warehouses, west elevation. *(Harris Library)*

Canal warehouses, east elevation. Taken from the Corn Exchange building,
between Fleet Street and Wharf Street. *(Harris Library)*

Coal sidings. *(Harris Library)*

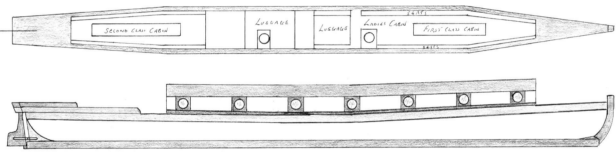

Packet Boat. *(Author)*

There was a substantial L-shaped basin at Preston, with warehouses, stables, wharves, branches and dry docks, stretching northward for a third of a mile, as far as Maudland Road bridge. When the railways came, the tram lines were replaced by standard gauge sidings, with wooden turntables and spurs to the various coal merchants yards. Manually operated coal tipping machinery was put in along the way for the transfer of coal from railway wagons to barges.

The boatman heaves-to with muscle, clogs, rope and capstan, while another 10 ton load of prime Wigan coal is tipped into the hold. *(Harris Library)*

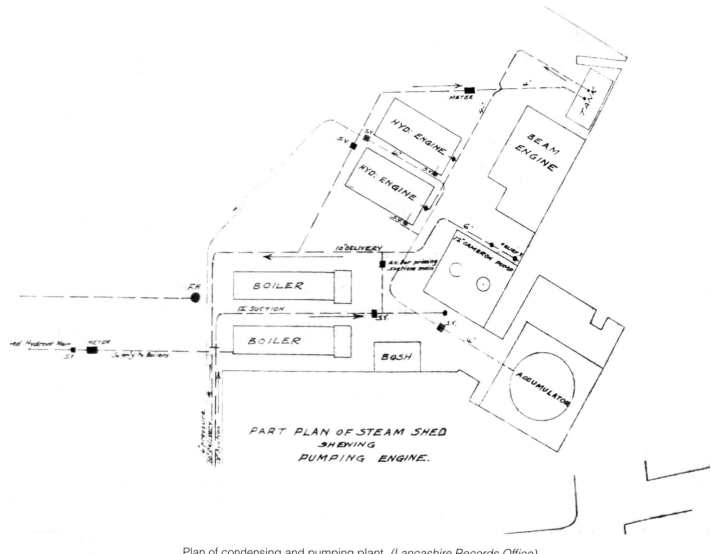

Plan of condensing and pumping plant. *(Lancashire Records Office)*

The Lancaster Canal Company Supplied water to the railway at Preston for the locomotive siphons, tanks and hydraulic lifts; the railway troughs at Salwick, Hest Bank and Brock, were also fed from the canal. A number of local textile mills, foundries and other industrial premises in the area had their water supplied from the same source. In 1886, for instance, we hear of water from the canal being condensed for use at Shelley Road Mill @ £81. 5s. per annum. The water was drawn from the canal at a location to the north of Fylde Road bridge, in the vicinity of Steam Mill. A twelve inch diameter cast-iron suction pipe followed the course of the railway to a condensing plant somewhere in the Maudland area, and from here the purified water was conveyed to the central station and beyond in a ten inch diameter pipe which terminated at the water tank adjacent to the No.1A signal box. A four inch diameter pipe branched off and continued south to serve a water column at the Preston end of the Ribble bridge. Other branch pipes of 4, 6 and 8 inches served the station water columns, the hydraulic accumulator in the south - east corner of Fishergate bridge and Christian Road warehouse.

Both the canal and railway companies patronised a local merchant by the name of James Todd, whose establishment was at 10 Lune Street, Preston, which was at that time, 3 doors away from Friargate. He was a Supplier of rope, twine, Hessian sacks and bags; Charles Macintosh Company's patent wagon and cart covers (as well as the famous waterproof coats); Stockholm tar and tarred oakum for ships and canal boats. He also Manufactured wagon covers to order. The firm of E. Bagnall Beddoe was in a convenient location at No. 4, Wharf Street (opposite the Corn Exchange) to do business with the canal company. They supplied bar iron, suitable for engineers, blacksmiths and wheelwrights; sheets, plates and cooper's hoops; horse-shoe iron, tip iron and nail rods; cast, shear, spring and blister steel; sperm, olive, neatsfoot, linseed and other industrial oils; colliery, locomotive and cart grease; varnish and paints. They were also agents for the Provincial (life) Insurance Company.

Marsh Lane bridge with the Boatmans pub in the left background. Notice how the track dips beneath the bridge, to allow for engines to pass under. This provision was made following a tragic accident, whereby the crew of a 'foreign' locomotive, who failed to see a warning notice, ran their engine beneath the bridge, where it became stuck with the steam whistle broken off. Both men were trapped in the cab and scalded to death by the escaping steam. *(Harris Library)*

1885 girder and plate bridge which carried the Longridge line at Maudland. *(Harris Museum)*

There was more than coal and timber to be had at the Preston wharves, for we read in an advertisement in the Chronicle edition for September 25, 1858, that a Mr. Henry Ashcroft, of No. 2, Pottery Hill, Preston, was offering for sale some 3,000 tons of night soil and street-sweepings (human excrement and horse manure mixed with ashes and rotting vegetables etc.), at a very reasonable rate. The fragrant heap was located at one of the wharves, where it could be 'conveniently conveyed to Lancaster, Kendal and all intermediate places, for use as fertilizer.' Mr. Ashcroft also opened a bone mill at Salwick, close to the canal, where he sold ground kitchen bones at £7 10s. Per ton. Imagine taking a slow boat to Kendal with that sort of stuff on board – and having to shovel and barrow it all out at journey's end!

## COAL YARD AT BAMBER BRIDGE,
# TO LET
### WITH IMMEDIATE POSSESSION,
**With** excellent **WEIGHING MACHINE**, Stage, Office, &c., Also,
## ON SALE BY PRIVATE TREATY

## 22 CANAL BOATS, AND 112 RAILWAY COAL WAGGONS.

**Several of the boats are entirely new, and of excellent workmanship, and the remainder are in good working condition. Twenty are lying on the South Level of the Lancaster Canal, at the Summit, and at Adlington, and two on the North Level at Preston. The Coal Waggons may be seen at the Coal Yard at Bamber Bridge.**
**Proposals in writing will be received by Mr. ALEXANDER BANNERMAN, South Cottage, Chorley, and of whom further particulars may be obtained.**

Preston Chronicle, March 1842.

An experiment was carried out at Preston on September 10, 1859, with a screw-driven steam boat. The engines, screw propeller, boiler, fittings and erection were manufactured and carried out by Messrs. Gadd and Hill, Regent Ironworks, Salford; and the locomotive boiler and iron boat were manufactured by Mr. Stevenson, Canal Foundry, Preston. The engine comprised two 10 ins. diameter cylinders, each having an 18 ins. stroke, giving a maximum of seventy revolutions per minute, and the screw propeller, 200 RPM. The propeller had three blades and measured 3ft. 3 ins. in diameter with a pitch of 5 ft. The boiler was 11 ft. in length by 3ft. 9 ins. diameter, and contained 52 fire tubes of 2 ½ ins. diameter. The fire grate had an area of 12 square feet, and the total length of the steam boat was 70ft. with a beam of 14 ft. 6 ins. The total weight including fuel was 28 tons, and the paying cargo, in addition to her machinery, was 24 tons of coals.

The boats towed by the steamer were six in number, each having a length of 70 ft. with a beam of 14 ft. 6 ins. The combined weight of the barges was 115 tons, carrying a combined weight of 296 tons 18 cwt. of coals, giving a total weight (inc. 52 tons on the steamer) of 463 tons 18cwt. She sailed comfortably at a rate of two miles in an hour and a half, with 55 pounds of steam on the square inch. After a distance of two miles, the steamer was detached and went astern past the barges. She was then attached and tugged them back to the basin, rudders leading, at the same speed. She would, in all probability, have been able to pull twice the number of barges, but the men of iron and steam were lucky to get the use of the original number after paying the boatmen 2 shillings each to partake in the experiment. Perhaps those who didn't offer their barges had visions of an unwelcome change in the scheme of things. The trial was witnessed by the managing director of the canal company, Mr. R.P. Gregson; Mr. J. Stevenson of Preston; the company agent, Mr. Thomas Proctor and Mr. J.F. Burgess of Messrs. Gadd & Hill, who proposed a second trial at a later date with a larger propeller. It would appear that nothing further was heard of the matter.

The L.N.W.R. bought all the property belonging to the Lancaster Canal for half a million pounds in 1885, and the canal company ceased to exist from January 1, 1886. The L.C.C. rights had been purchased back in 1867, when the company also owned sea-going vessels that plied between Glasson and Glasgow, specialising in heavy goods such as stone, timber, sugar and treacle at 8s. per ton. The L.N.W. intended to fill in the canal basin at Preston, together with a section from there to Greenbank, and build a large wharf with sidings at Garstang for the transshipment of coal. The idea was deemed to be impracticable.

Ladywell Street wharves. *(Harris Library)*

## Steam Saw Mill Company

The company was formed in 1836, with the first 12 months spent in dealing with bulk timber, erecting the building and setting up the cutting equipment. The company began cutting timber in 1837, and difficulties arose for a time, consequent upon the introduction of machinery and the attitude of the people with their violent opposition to mechanical appliances. Indeed, the proprietors had kept a souvenir of those dark days, in the form of a blunderbuss, which had been used during the course of an attack upon the premises. The works chimney had a singular incident connected with its construction. Upon its completion, and for some unaccountable reason, one of the workmen was left on top after the scaffolding had been removed. He solved the problem of getting back down by unravelling his worsted stockings, letting down the thread to which a cord was attached, and hauling the cord up. He then secured the cord and with it, he hauled up a substantial length of stout rope. He then secured the rope to the chimney, and let himself down safely to terra firma, much to the delight of a large crowd of onlookers. The directors in 1885 were James Robinson, Adam Leigh, Dr. Brown and Robert Gregson. It is through the courtesy of the last mentioned person that permission was granted for the works to be thoroughly inspected and recorded. The mill was located in Bridge Lane, being bounded respectively by Maudland road, Leighton Street, the canal and Bridge Lane.

Entrance to B.R. Ladywell House. *(W. Kidson for British Railways Board)*

Another view of Ladywell House from Heatley Street. The stone building on the corner with Ladywell Street was a canal warehouse. The wall on the left borders the site of the once extensive coal sidings at Corporation Street. *(W. Kidson for British Railways Board)*

The works covered an extensive area, with the Lancaster Canal skirting the full length of the yard. At the top end of the yard and nearest to Maudland Road, a short branch from the canal was constructed for the purpose of discharging log timber, and a powerful swing crane, at the edge of the wharf, was used for this purpose. The general yard was provided with two overhead travelling cranes and tram lines for the hoisting and removal of heavy timber, and some years later, a short siding was taken off the Maudland curve to serve the mill, which terminated beneath an overhead steam-crane gantry. The firm also carried out its own lath rending in spacious workshops near the wharf. Rending required great skill and dexterity with knives or small hatchets, and an expert could earn a good wage out of the trade. The yards were well stocked with almost every variety of timber: oak, birch, deal, baywood, mahogany, &c., and most of it was landed at Glasson Dock, where the firm possessed extensive storage premises. From Glasson, the timber was brought to Preston by boats or flats on the canal. Flooring timber came principally from Norway; oak, elm, ash and spruce deals from Nova Scotia; pitch pine from Pensacola, South America, and mahogany from the West Indies.

Looking west down Marsh Lane, the stables entrance for the Boatman's public house is on the left, with the north end of Ladywell House just visible. Beyond this are the canal bridge and old warehouses. *(W. Kidson for British Railways Board)*

Looking from Marsh Lane and the junction with Ladywell Street. The main coal office was situated between the wall and the B.R. Offices. *(W. Kidson for British Railways Board)*

The yard handled between 15,000 to 20,000 tons of timber per year. Inside the steam saw shed, the first machine encountered was the deal-frame, which cut the deal into specific lengths and thicknesses for use in making packing cases. Close by was a planking machine, which could also tongue, groove, mould and fashion anything a machine of its class could have been expected to do. There were rack benches for running the logs from the yard to the sawing machine, where they were scraped, chipped and dogged. There was a sharpening shop, where the blades had fine cutting edges restored to them by an ingenious piece of machinery, which incorporated a steam-driven emery wheel, the teeth being finished off by a bevelled emery wheel. There was a blacksmith's shop with forge and steam-driven fan, and an engineer's department, where all the patterns and machine tools were manufactured, and a machine which was invented and assembled by one of the engineers for sharpening the most intricate knives or irons, which were used in the more artistic and decorative mouldings. The emery wheels were cooled by water which was pumped from tanks at the back of the machine. Components for the boilers and steam engines were also fabricated in the engineer's workshop. The engine house was a lofty structure, well illuminated and pleasant in appearance with whitewashed walls and well polished machinery. The floor was decked with best quality lattice wood. There was a small, vertical steam engine with inverted cylinder, which drove the machinery in the sharpening and engineer's department's and the blacksmith's fan. The chief engine for driving the mill's heavy machinery was a very large beam engine with a 24 ft. diameter fly-wheel; the stroke was 6 ft. and the engine was fitted with a governor and cut-off valve. The boiler was 27 ft. in length by 7 ft. 6 ins. diameter, and was capable of working up to a very high pressure, the water being fed into it by a force-pump, with a valve for regulating supply. The capacious upper part of the boiler house was used for drying timber, the seasoning of which was thoroughly understood by the firm and most carefully attended to in respect of every type of timber on the premises.

A.P.T. 25200 & 252001 undergoing trials at Dock Street with brochure and ticket. *(Walter Thompson)*

Most of the machinery was located in the 'dark regions' below the engine house, where there were huge crank-driven drums, belts and pulleys for driving the horizontal and circular saws. Some of the iron drums were 2 ft. wide by 6 ft. in diameter, with belting of corresponding size. Each counter shaft had a fly wheel in connection with the frame, and one of the larger cranks measured 4 ft. 6 ins. across the segment and 6 ½ ins. broad. The cranks were cast hollow and filled with lead to counterbalance the weight of the frame working above. The fly wheels were also cast hollow for the purpose of being weighted when necessary. There was sufficient power in this subterranean transmission house to drive with ease as many as fifty saws in one frame. The No. 1 frame had the capacity to cut logs of 2 ft. 10 ins. by 2 ft. 7 ins. deep ; No. 2 frame, 2 ft. wide by 23 ins., and No. 3 frame had a similar capacity. There was machinery for cutting flitches (broad boards cut into smaller dimensions), and driving a rack bench, which was used for cutting all kinds of round timber. The saws for this kind of work were 5 ft. 6 ins. in diameter, with 4 ins. tooth pitch. Pulleys and gears were used to obtain the requisite speed for each kind of work. Another remarkable machine was used to plane top and bottom and tongue and groove the sides of boards at the rate of 13 ft. per minute. The sawdust and chippings were conveyed into a hopper, with bags placed beneath ready to be filled and sent off to customers. There was also a moulding shop with instruments and machinery for making 'sweeps', or circular cuts for cart-wheels and other radiused pieces for church and other windows.

A line up of modern traction and rolling stock at the eastern limit of Dock Street sidings. The Ladywell staff car park was constructed on the site of the filled-in canal basin. *(Courtesy, Stephen Dowle)*

A group of drivers from the Preston Branch of ASLEF, taking part in the Guild parade of 1972.
From left to right: Ted Aspin, Robert (Jock) Cummings, Steve Bennett, Arthur Chester, Dave Hogarth,
Roy (Chalky) White, Geoff Ford, Jimmy Clayton, Harry Robinson, Jimmy Boyle, Brian Fare, Dennis Leech,
Wilf Buckley, Frank Herdman. The gathering took place on a street off new Hall Lane.
*(Lancashire Evening Post)*

# Canal Foundry

John Stevenson took over the business from the Earl of Balcarres in 1833[1], and carried it on with great success up to the time of his death in 1872, when it passed into the hands of Charles and Hutton Birley, who invested huge sums of money in new buildings and plant. The company's premises were located between the Lancaster & Preston Railway and Dock Street. Just about every kind of mechanical contrivance, large and small was was made here, from founding to machining, and mill gearing was a speciality with the main clients being Horrockses, Miller and Co., and other large mills in the Preston area. The foundry was one of the first to manufacture the new double-helical-toothed gearing, and steel making plant for gas-fired boilers. The erecting shop was quite spacious, with three overhead cranes capable of lifting 15 tons each. The machine shop was well worth a visit, as it was full of huge steam-driven lathes, planers and an hydraulic press. One of the lathes was capable of turning components of up to 14 ft. in diameter, and the largest planing machine could cope with articles up to 8 ft. square by 20ft. long. Machinery was also made for the manufacture of gunpowder, whereby the powder was taken from an hydraulic press in the form of a cake, and then broken up by a series of brass rollers. The foundry itself was big enough to make the largest castings, with moulds for hydraulic rams and winding wheels of up to 20 ft. diameter; it would have been a particularly noisy place with roaring furnaces and the pounding of steam hammers etc. The iron store was once the site of an old monastery which had connections with Tulketh Hall Priory and Furness Abbey; as the decades rolled by it became part of a barracks, then a house of correction, and continued as such until the prison at the east end of Church Street was opened in 1790. The monastery's sundial, bearing the legend 'Dum spectas Fugio,' (Whilst thou lookest I fly) had been rescued and was fixed above one of the foundry windows.

Driver Walter Thompson, signs off at Dock Street, at the end of his last duty before retirement at 65, on July 19, 1981. He had brought the Brush Type 2 loco, 47 462, back from Crewe. *(Courtesy, W. Thompson)*

Of particular interest was the fact that the L.N.W. line to Lancaster passed close to the works by way of a viaduct, and some of the arches were utilised by the company as dressing sheds for castings and store-rooms for miscellaneous articles such as patterns and timber etc. One of the arches provided a garage for the company's traction engine, which was used for carrying heavy boilers from the works to their destinations within the town, or to one of the railway goods stations. Prior to this mode of transport, the boilers were carried on wooden carts drawn by horses. The Preston Chronicle relates that on Thursday, August 7, 1845, such a conveyance with a large boiler weighing some 15 tons, was proceeding up Fishergate at around 7 a.m. when, on reaching the tramroad tunnel, one of the back wheels broke. The horses were unhooked and work was carried out to replace the wheel and strengthen the cart, which wasn't completed until 6 a.m. the following morning. A team of 16 strong horses was yoked-up and the cumbersome load continued on its way up Fishergate, then down Lune Street and on to Friargate, where it was found necessary to remove three yards of stone wall before it could enter the yard of Mr. Hawkins's factory.[2]

The foundry was closed down on Friday, December 18, 1891, and on the following evening, the employees assembled at the North Western Hotel for a farewell dinner and the presentation of time-pieces and illuminated testimonials to Mr. J.T. Southworth, foreman of the works, and Mr. Mitchell, foreman of the boiler-making department. Most of the machinery was purchased by Messrs. Friedenthall for use at their premises on Fylde Road. The buildings were purchased by the L.N.W.R. and demolished to make way for sidings and a proposed widening of the main line, which came too late to avoid the derailment of the Scotch Express in that area some 5 years later.

# Canal Coal Merchants 1880's

Bridge Lane, Pearson Knowles Coal & Iron Co. Bridge Lane.

Smethurst, Hoyle & Grime. Bridge Lane.

Hugh Snape. Greenbank Street.

W & J Turner. Fleet Street.

Wigan Coal & Iron, at Wharf Street, Ladywell Street and Fletcher Road.

Spring Colliery Coal Depot, Bridge Lane, Preston. (1854).

Thomas Pearson was proprietor of Arley Mine Coal Pit, which supplied first class coals for domestic purposes, giving clean fires, especially suited for parlours and sitting rooms. The slack from the above coal was quite suitable for smithy purposes. Also there were Ince 4ft. and 5ft. coals; along with the 9 feet and trencher Bone coals, the latter being extensively used and approved for steam purposes, and in the burning of tiles, bricks etc.
There was also a constant supply of Ince Engine slack on hand; also smithy and engine coke.
John Furness, agent.

Bradley Colliery had its own coal yard on the east bank, at a yearly rate of £ 84 19s. (Jan 19, 1850).

Byrom, Taylor and Byrom, coal proprietors, Bridge Lane. The yard was adjacent to the entrance to the basin. (August 1851)

John Darlington opened a warehouse on the old quay wharf at Marsh End, He also had a coal office on Ladywell Street. (March 25, 1848).

Ince Hall Coal & Cannel Company, No 1 Coal Wharf, Fishergate. Edward Hemingway, Agent.(1859).

The Coal Consumer's Company, Office & yard, Barrack Street, Marsh Lane, for Wallsend, Orrel, Arley, King and Yard Coal for parlour & kitchen; also Burgy and slack for engine fuel. (1874).

Thomas Turner, 3 Ladywell Street, Specialist in Orrell coal (1859).

B & R Fisher, Coal Proprietors, Bradley Hall Collieries, Wigan
Yard & Office, Bridge Lane. Also Lime Burners, Greenbank Lime Works. J. Turner, Agent (1887).

Richard Evans & Co. (late Whitehead's), for Haydock, Ashton, Edge Green and Park Collieries. Commenced business on 30th March 1878 at Bridge Lane coal yard. Household, engines and shipping. Best steam slack.

Jabez Kay & Co. Coal merchants and colliery agents. Barracks Street, Bridge Lane (1892). House-fire, furnace and steam coal.

James Turner & Co. Coal merchants and colliery agents. Offices, 12 Lune Street.(1885).
Gas coal & cannel, contractors & shippers. House coal from 6d. To 9d. per cwt. Wagon loads supplied to any railway siding at wholesale prices.

John Darlington had a coal office at No. 17, Ladywell Street and opened a warehouse on the old quay wharf at Marsh End in 1848. He was agent for Welch, Whittle, Blainscough Hall and Wigan Collieries.

## FOOTNOTES

(1) James Lindsey, 24th Earl of Crawford and 7th Earl of Balcarres, 1783-1869. He lived at Haigh Hall near Wigan, where his family owned Haigh Colliery and subsequently founded the Wigan Coal & Iron Company.

(2) Preston Chronicle, August 9, 1845.

# CHAPTER THREE

# The Dock Branch

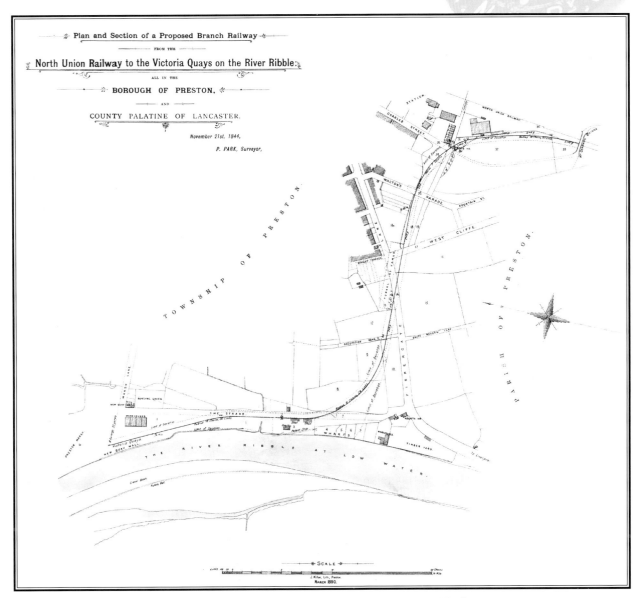

1844 plan of Dock Branch. *(Richard Parker archive)*

The Ribble Navigation Company was quick to recognise the potential of the new railway at Preston, and this enthusiasm was reciprocated by the North Union, who obtained an act to build a railway to the Victoria Quay on the Ribble. A clause in the Act stated that it had to operate as a separate company called the Ribble Branch Railway. The line was completed and opened for traffic on Thursday, July 16, 1846; the single line branched off the N.U. at a point close to German's Bridge at the south end of the station and descended a severe gradient on a curve with a radius of 8 chains (528 ft.), the steepest section of which was 1 in 29. Then came a tunnel of 145 yards, which ran beneath Fishergate at an angle, after which the gradient eased off and the line reached the dock by way of an angled level crossing over Strand Road. From the west side of this road, it became the property of the navigation company. The only over-bridge on the line was built some time later between the west portal of the tunnel and Strand Road, for the convenience of a Mr. Pedder.

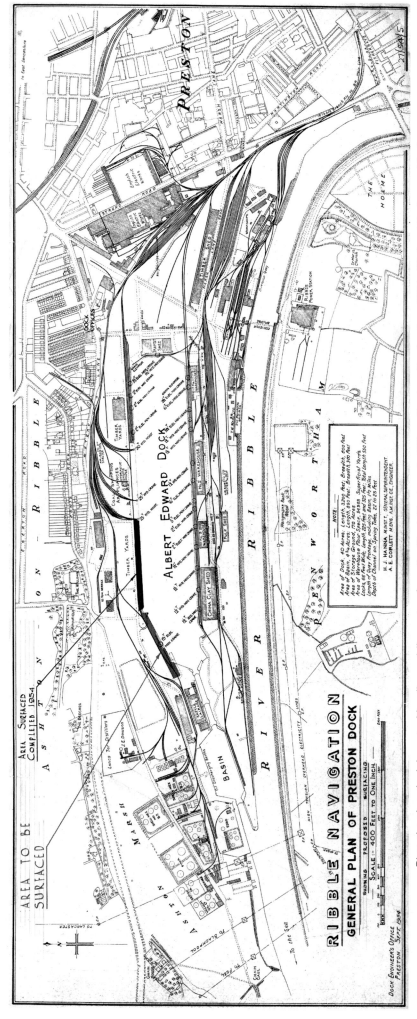

Plan showing dock layout with railway sidings etc., from the Dock Engineer's Office, Preston, September 1954. *(Richard Parker archive)*

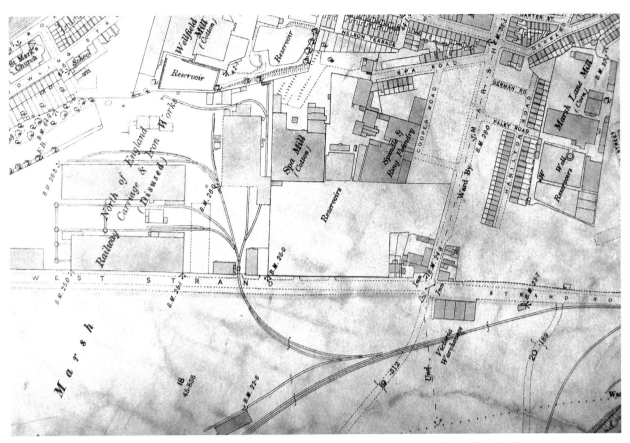

1892 map showing North of England Carriage & Wagon Works premises. *(Harris Library)*

Later on, a siding was taken off to serve Allsup's ship yard, and a connection was made just to the north of the bonded warehouse to serve the North of England Carriage & Wagon Works on the east side of Strand Road. This was a large complex of about 60,904 square yards where, apart from railway rolling stock, the company manufactured iron merchant bars, plates, sheets and tip iron. There were powerful steam hammers, furnaces and tools for making axles, shafts, iron gates, hurdles, wheel hoops and many other types of scrap forgings. The iron department was capable of turning out 370 to 400 tons of finished work every week and the railway department could turn out an average of 60 wagons per week including 60 to 70 sets of wheels and axles. The large open spaces within the works were ideal for the manufacture of iron bridges and roofing. In 1878, the company announced that it was in financial difficulties, and that it was unable to pay the £500 annual ground rent to Preston Corporation. The company was wound up and the site put up for sale on July 12, 1879.[1]

Preston Corporation took over from the Ribble navigation Company in 1882, and commenced a ten year development of the site, whereby the the course of the Ribble was diverted to make room for the construction of a 40 acre dock. The Albert Edward Dock, as it became known, was opened in 1892, and boasted one and a half miles of wharf accommodation and 25 miles of railway tracks and sidings. The principal cargoes comprised bananas, china clay, timber, pulp and petroleum. By the 1950's, some 2,500 wagons were moved in each direction every week, and no fewer than 150 coal wagons were taken down the branch on a daily basis, to provide fuel for the power station across the river. This involved some 12 trips a day up and down, with a banker on the return trips; the motive power comprising for the most part class G7 Super D's. The allocation of Dock locomotives over the years was dominated by six-coupled saddle tanks and, as time was running out for steam traction in the 1960's, the last stand was made by the Bagnall and Barclay types with outside cylinders, some of which were endowed with business-like names, 'Energy', 'Enterprise', 'Progress', 'Courageous', 'Conqueror' and 'Princess'. There was also a fireless loco called Duke, which worked in areas where flammable liquids were stored. Diesel traction took over in 1968, and the only steam locomotive to survive was Princess, which was preserved by the Lakeside Railway Society. The dock closed in 1979, and the site was redeveloped for retail units and residential property, with the dock itself being transformed into a marina for leisure craft. The dock branch is still used for the passage of tanker trains to and from a bitumen refinery, and a section of the line from the marina up to Strand Road is used by the Ribble Steam Railway, which has a wonderful assortment of preserved steam locomotives and rolling stock.

Class 08 shunter, D3368, emerges from the subterranean section of the branch
on September 13, 1960. *(Tony Gillett)*

A nameless four-coupled RSH saddle tank, not dissimilar to an ex - L.Y.R. 'Pug', stands
among the barrels and trailers on February 28, 1961. *(Tony Gillett)*

A beautiful portrait of energy at rest. *(Arthur Haymes)*

Perseverance has buried her nose in the shed and she's not coming out for anyone until she's got some make-up on; a lengthy process involving the application of red paint to the buffer beams and a bit of fancy work on the smoke box door. *(Arthur Haymes)*

Saddle tanks, Courageous and Perseverance between duties on May 5, 1961.
Note the spark-arrestors atop the chimneys. *(Tony Gillett)*

Strand Road signal cabin with L.N.W. ground frame and track diagram.
Of interest are the B.R. Standard telephone bell, and the number 69 on the gable. *(Author's collection)*

## FOOTNOTES

[1] In 1896, the complex was reopened for use by the Electric Railway and Tramway Carriage Works, by two remarkable Glaswegian entrepreneurs, W.B. Dick and John Kerr. Two years later the company amalgamated with the Manchester firm of Equipment Syndicate and commenced erecting new workshops on both sides of Strand Road. In 1903 it became Dick Kerr and Co.; and in 1905 the name changed again to the United Electric Car Company, which lasted until 1918, when it became part of the English Electric company. In 1969 it was absorbed into the General Electric Company.

# CHAPTER FOUR
# Central Station

A 1920's aerial view from the south, showing the extent of the goods yard at Christian Road. *(British Railways Board)*

A view of the much attenuated layout in 2011.
*(Chris Powell)*

The North Union station building had come in for a lot of criticism since its opening in 1838 and, notwithstanding some minor improvements carried out in the 1840's, was barely able to cope with the volume of traffic and growing number of passengers following the the arrival of the lines from Lancaster, Fleetwood, Bolton and Liverpool. There had been much congestion, leading to protracted delays, and the staff had to work hard and fast in order to get one train out of the way and make room for another, while coping at the same time with shunting, stock movements and intermittent coal and goods traffic. Accidents involving staff and passengers alike were inevitable and of a frequent occurrence, especially during the hours of darkness, with many resulting in mutilations and fatalities. Something needed to be done, and in April 1854, the lessees of the N.U. appointed Mr. Norris, civil engineer of the L.N.W.R. and Mr.

Meek, civil engineer of the L.Y.R. to commence a survey for the extension of the station and for the accommodation of additional lines, platforms and offices on the west side. The estimated cost for all this was £50,000 to £70,000. At the same time, the N.U. was engaged in the construction of a siding some 458 yards in length on the south end of the Ribble bridge. This was intended to keep goods traffic off the main lines, thus preventing the delays to passenger trains. They were later expanded by the L.N.W.R and became known as 'Ribble Sidings.'

The delapidated station shed as seen from Fishergate.
Demolition work appears to have begun on the west side. *(Harris Museum)*

The new Fishergate bridge is taking shape, and most
of the tunnel has been demolished. *(Harris Museum)*

The station improvements were completed some months later, increasing the number of tracks to six, with two more island platforms. Unfortunately it proved to be an ineffective remedy for the growing congestion problems. The arrival of the East Lancashire Railway's Preston Extension in 1850 did not affect the volume of traffic in the station, as the company had its own platforms and goods yard on the Butler Street side; however, it was inevitable, that the increasing number of passengers arriving from the East Lancashire townships and booking to travel further north and south, would add considerably to the dangerous crowding on the narrow platforms; furthermore, passengers continued to cross the tracks on the level in order to get to the N.U. trains in time, rather than use a narrow footbridge at the south end of the station, which did not provide access to the island platforms in any case. Accidents followed thick and fast, with members of staff suffering the most. The station platforms and buildings often presented scenes of depravity and iniquity; the general refreshment rooms, for example, were frequented by loungers, spongers, card sharps, prostitutes and spivs; the crowded platforms provided a happy hunting ground for the ubiquitous pick-pockets, and there was also the opportunist theft of passengers' luggage and railway property including mailbags. Added to this were the occasional dramatic scenes of wanted criminals being apprehended on the platforms; drunken and riotous behaviour among servicemen and sporting types; the remarkable escapades of fare-dodgers, vicious assaults on station officials and the never-ending lamentations of those who's trains were either delayed or cancelled.

The 2nd and 3rd class waiting rooms left just as much to be desired, and it took some courage on the part of the traveller to enter such places, as much the same examples of human kind could be found here as in the refreshment rooms; and the stench alone must have been enough to put the more sensitive element off crossing the threshold. One would have had to contend with the lavender fragrance of stale alcohol and tobacco fumes, bad breath, human and animal waste and the almost audible odour of unwashed, vermin-riddled bodies and clothing. One must bear in mind also, that whenever accidents occurred in the vicinity of the station, the victims were usually carried to one of these rooms and laid on a large wooden table, where they could be attended to by the company surgeon. Emergency amputations weren't uncommon, and corpses were often laid out on these tables in readiness for a coroner's examination. The waiting rooms also became popular depositories for unwanted babies, and it is recorded that in March, 1880, a porter who discovered a new born baby, had decided to take it home to his wife and adopt it. Once this act of benevolence had become known to the wider public, the station master, Mr. Miles, began to receive many letters from anonymous Prestonians, asking him if any more of his porters would like to adopt unwanted children.[1]

On October 6, 1860, the first arrest at the station by means of telegraphic communication took place. The Preston Police received a message from Superintendent Little, of Whitehaven, stating that a female named Florence Robinson, 18 years of age, had proceeded by the 11 o'clock train from there to Preston with eight stolen sovereigns in her possession, and requested that the girl be detained upon her arrival at the station. The telegram also contained a description of the girl. An officer was then sent to the station and, on the arrival of the train, the fugitive was 'eyed' in the act of stepping out of a carriage. The officer then proceeded up to her and informed her of his errand. She was quite astonished, and afterwards explained that she had taken the money from her aunt. She was taken to the Police Station where the sum of £7 5s. was found in her possession. A message was then telegraphed to Whitehaven and the prisoner was remanded until the arrival of an officer from Whitehaven, who took her back in the course of the day.[2]

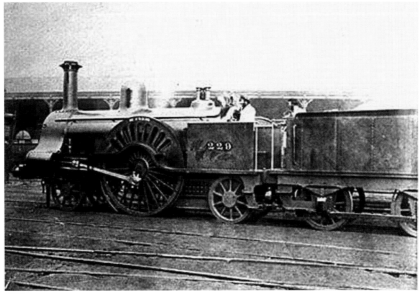

L.N.W. 'Bloomer' No. 229, at the south end of the old N.U. station. (Harris Museum)

The scene at Preston wasn't all derision, knavery, chaos and carnage; there were moments when bouts of honesty and civility broke out, and one such outstanding example occurred on Saturday, August 30, 1879, when a passenger managed to lose £600 consisting of five £100 notes, one £50 note and the rest in gold and silver. An honest grocer's out-porter, James Day, employed by Carter &co., at the market place, discovered the lost treasure and handed it over to Mr. Miles. The 'gentleman' who carelessly mislaid the money, promptly rewarded the young lad with the grand sum of one shilling, and left the authorities wondering whether the generous requital was likely to encourage honesty or thieving.

L.N.W. 2222, Sir Gilbert Claughton takes water at the north end, circa 1914. *(H. Gordon Tidy)*

L.N.W. 2222, Sir Gilbert Claughton with a down train, circa 1914. *(H. Gordon Tidy)*

# Yolland Report of July 18th, 1866 [3]

On Tuesday, February 20, 1866, a train carrying a large industrial boiler passed through the station. with the 'overhang' being well over gauge and, inevitably, the boiler collided with one of the tubular iron roof supports, knocking a chunk out of it. The following Thursday, a train entered the station with a consignment of iron bars. The load on one of the wagons had shifted and one or two of the bars came into contact with the already damaged roof support, breaking it in two.

It was these two incidents, coupled together with numerous other issues connected with the station that prompted Colonel William Yolland to carry out a thorough examination of the premises on behalf of the Board of Trade. His report was submitted to the Board on July 18, 1866, and runs as follows:

"The Preston station, which is complained of by the memorialists, is divided into parts: one on the south-eastern side, owned exclusively by the East Lancashire and represented by the Lancashire and Yorkshire Railway Company, and the other by the North Union Railway Company, and now owned by the London & North Western and Lancashire & Yorkshire Railway Companies namely, in the proportion of two-thirds and one-third respectively. Both companies own land to the north of Fishergate and the LNWR have recently acquired the Lancaster Canal property. The Ribble branch, west of the station is owned by the joint railway companies and the Ribble Navigation Company in equal moieties.

The North Union goods yard is situated at the south western angle of the station and is entered from German's Bridge at the south extremity of the station, and its length is so limited that the marshalling and shunting of goods trains can only be done by fouling the main lines, by which the trains enter and leave the station. The passenger platforms commence about 80 yards south of Fishergate, which is passed under by a tunnel of about the same length, with two lines of way only through it. From Fishergate on the north to German's Bridge at the south, is nearly a quarter of a mile in length. There are six lines of railway passing between the platforms used by passengers at the north end of the station, and the two lines through the tunnel are made use of for shunting and making up passenger trains. The two centre lines are the main up and down lines from north to south. There are three platforms to the west and two east of the main lines; but the most important and best platforms are on the western and eastern sides of the station, respectively of 156 and 97 yards in length, and that on the eastern side is continued on a curve in a south-easterly direction for the East Lancashire passenger traffic, and is 186 yards in length, 1 foot high and 14 ½ feet wide. This East Lancashire platform is partly covered in, the roof being supported on one side by pillars placed in the 6 feet space between the adjacent lines. The western platform is about 11 inches above the level of the rails, and 11 ½ feet wide opposite the booking office, but this space is narrowed to 9 feet opposite the book-stall. The eastern platform is of the same height, and 18 ½ feet wide opposite to the booking office, and 16 feet 8 inches opposite to the book-stall. These are fair platforms, but objectionable on account of their height, and the western one is long enough to accommodate the greater proportion of trains that are run.

As far as I could learn, it would seem that these eastern and western platforms only have been approved by way of the inspectors of the Board of Trade. The next platform on the western side is 133 yards in length, 11 inches high, and placed between two adjacent lines of railway. It is only 6 feet 2 inches wide at the broadest part, and the width is diminished at the north end by some pillars to support the roof, leaving only about 3 feet 6 inches as the distance between the side of the pillars and the edge of the platform. The next platform, on the western side, next the main down line, is still more objectionable and dangerous. It is placed between adjacent lines of railway and it is only 50 yards in length, 14 inches high and 3 feet wide, and even this width is not clear, as there are three pillars supporting the roof on this platform, leaving only 20 inches space between the sides and the edge of the platform.

The remaining platform, which has not yet been described, is 112 yards in length, 14 feet wide and 2 foot high, and it is separated from the platform on the eastern side of the station, before referred to, by a single line of rails. There is a row of pillars on this platform, 17 in number, towards the western side, from which the carriages are entered, and the distance between the sides of the pillars and the edges of the platform varies from 4 feet 6 inches to 4 feet 10 inches. Another series of pillars, 11 in number, are placed north of and in continuation of those on the platform, 3 feet wide between two adjacent lines of railway, so that the sides of the pillars are distant from 2 feet 6 inches to 2 feet 9 inches from the rails on one side, and from 3 feet 10 inches to 4 feet 1 inch on the other. A foot bridge is provided to cross from the eastern to the western platforms, but to get to any of the other platforms, the rails must be crossed on the level.

Preston Station is admitted to be a wretched station, and the propriety of constructing a new one has been under consideration for a large number of years.

The railway companies before referred to, own a large portion of the land that would be required in the formation of a new station, but it is possible that they may require some additional land to enable a good station to be constructed, adequate for the large amount of traffic that passes through it. According to the general manager, 71 passenger, goods and coal trains arrive at Preston from the north, and mostly pass on, while 63 similar trains arrive from the south and mostly pass on; and during the Whitsun week, about 90 special trains arrived at and left Preston Station, in addition to the ordinary trains just enumerated.

There have not been many casualties to passengers at this station, but a good many of the company's servants have, in the course of years, been killed or injured; but more, however, than might have been expected from the extent of the traffic. No complaints are made of any want of attention on the part of the inspectors or servants of the railway companies employed at this station, but all parties seem to agree in stating that great care is exercised in conducting the traffic.

I am informed that both the London & North Western and the Lancashire & Yorkshire Railway Companies are anxious to have a new station constructed, but they cannot agree as to the proportion in which they should contribute funds to carry on the work; but after submitting the necessity for a new station, it appears to me that the amount each should contribute might properly be referred to an arbitrator to determine. As regards your instruction to report on any alterations that may be expedient and practicable, I have only to state that an entirely new station is required, and that I cannot recommend that any of the existing platforms, objectionable as some of them are, should be removed, as that would only tend to increase the danger. Additional length of platform accommodation is required, involving an additional length of station yard, which may be partly gained by running more lines beneath Fishergate; and it would be highly desirable, entirely to remove the goods stations to some other site in the town.

At the present time, some of the East Lancashire trains are actually obliged, occasionally, to discharge their passengers altogether away from any platform. If the two railway companies do not proceed, without delay, to agree respecting the construction of the new station, it may be expedient for their Lordships to withhold their sanction to any of the cheap train arrangements of these two companies for trains passing into or through Preston station as proper accommodation is certainly not provided, and the travelling public are subject to unusual risk."

In the light of this report, the L.N.W. and L.Y.R. Companies were empowered by an act of Parliament, in 1870, to enlarge and improve their station, demolish the tunnel at the north end and replace it with a substantial iron bridge.

About a month after the report was published, on August 14, another incident occurred at the station, as if to emphasise Colonel Yolland's damning conclusions with a clap of God-like thunder. A large section of the roof on the east side, measuring some 120 ft. by 5 ft., carrying several panes of thick plate glass and a heavy iron water pipe,suddenly collapsed without any warning. The noise was immense, and for a time it was thought that an explosion had taken place. This particular part of the station was usually crowded at that time, but on this occasion it was strangely quiet. Two porters, Oliver Beardsworth and Thomas Norris, and a woman with a child were sitting on the platform benches beneath the roof. Beardsworth was seriously injured and was attended to by Mr. Howitt, a local surgeon. Norris was also hurt, but his injuries were not in any way serious. The woman was slightly injured and the child escaped without a scratch. The broken roof support wasn't mentioned at the subsequent enquiry and the cause of the collapse was attributed to corroded iron nuts and bolts which secured the roof to the girder, and the defective joints having been further loosened by the recent high winds.

Preston Chronicle, June 8, 1871.

The dilapidated and dangerous old station remained as it was for some six years following the parliamentary act of 1870 and, notwithstanding the fact that a contractor had been engaged to commence demolition work in 1872, there continued, in the duration of that period, to be many accidents in which railwaymen were either killed or maimed for life, with little or no compensation for their wives and families. It was a shameful indictment on the parsimonious and greedy railway management of those dark and merciless times; for there was nothing pleasant about the lot of the working people in 19th century Britain. The environment these people found themselves in was sometimes fascinating and sometimes tolerable, but certainly not pleasant under any circumstances. And so the butcher's bill increased, until what appears to have been the last and particularly heavy straw was laid upon the camel's back:

### George Eckersley's death. Jan 3, 1876

#### Attributed to the wretched state of the station

Early on Monday morning, January 3, 1876, senior inspector, George Eckersley, met with a shocking death upon the railway. Shortly after 4 o'clock in the morning, he had to cross the line for the purpose of attending to the Manchester portion of a train for the north, and whilst in the act of crossing, he was struck and knocked down by a tank locomotive passing in the opposite direction and killed almost instantly. The driver shut off steam at Dock Street as there was a decline from that point to German's Bridge; this class of engines being of a particularly compact design, run noiselessly and it is conjectured that Mr. Eckersley never saw nor heard the approach of the engine.

The remains of the deceased, who was 57 years of age, 34 of which he had passed at Preston railway station, were carried to a waiting room on the east side of the building to await the inquest, which took place that evening at the North Western Hotel. Mr. Gilbertson, coroner, presided over the inquest and called upon John Ward, a gas fitter at the station of 71 Oxford Street, and son-in-law of the deceased, to identify the body. William Hodgson, of 10 Mount Street, an engine driver for the LNWR, stated that he was driving a shunting engine, number 518, from the company's engine shed at Maudland to the goods yard at German's Bridge. He had left Maudland at 4 o'clock and had seen nothing until he approached the wooden footway (level crossing) at the north end of the station, where he saw a man

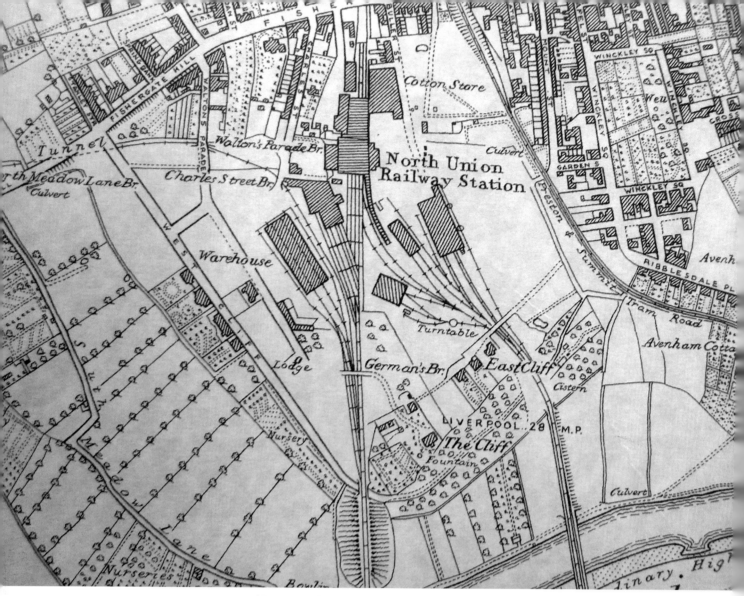

1850 map of Preston Station. *(Author's collection)*

step between the line of rails upon which the engine was running. At this point, the man could not have been above three or four yards ahead of the engine and was crossing the line a little to the south of the footway. The driver was sure the engine had hit him, and accordingly applied the brakes and stopped some 20 or 30 yards distant. He was not sure as to what speed he was going, but shut off steam at Dock Street and sounded the steam whistle at Stevenson's Foundry and again at Fishergate tunnel. He mentioned that there were written orders against excessive use of the whistle on the notice board at the shed. He climbed down and found the inspector lying face down and still, his right leg being some three yards from the body (The wheels had severed both legs). He then went to the platform and told the porter there what had happened.

Robert Kellett was stoker on the engine that had been waiting on the west side of the station to couple up and take the northbound train out. Mr. Eckersley asked him where his mate (the driver) was, and he told him he was on the other side of the station to see if he could find the train that they were scheduled to take out. Mr Eckersley explained to him that the train was about 40 minutes late and that the engine had broken down at Tyldsley, and that Kellett and his driver would have to take the train through to Carlisle. He then left Kellett and crossed over to the Butler Street side of the station. The Manchester train arrived shortly after, and he then saw someone crossing the line about 10 yards south of the wooden level crossing. He then remembered seeing the bright lamplight of the shunting engine and heard its steam whistle as it emerged from the Fishergate tunnel. He wasn't sure if the man had tried to step back out of the way of the engine, but he was dangerously close to it as it cleared the tunnel. As the engine passed through the station, he noticed smoke rising from the body of a man on the track. The porters arrived with their hand lamps and identified the body as that of Mr. Eckersley.

Summing up, the coroner said that nearly 6 years had passed since an act of Parliament was obtained to enable the railway companies to erect a new station, and yet little more than a year's work has been done. Criticism was levelled at the cramped conditions at the station and the dangerous level crossing from the east side to the temporary station buildings at Charles Street. It was this accident which led to a speeding up of work on the new station.

On Jan 8, a fund was set up to help Mr. Eckersley's widow and family. 'The integrity, assiduity and uniform courtesy which Inspector Eckersley manifested in the discharge of his official duties towards all classes for nearly 20 years earned for him a high measure of respect, and his death, caused as it was by a convergence of circumstances, removing it entirely from the ordinary category of railway fatalities, was deeply and universally regretted'.

Contributions were to be sent to the honorary secretaries, R. F. Easterby, County treasurer's office; George Wood, North Union Goods Department; Mr. Miles, Station Master; Mr. Lomax, Assistant Station Master; and Mr. Bowling, refreshment Rooms, Preston station; and all the newspaper offices.

The funeral procession set off from his residence on Bolton Street West shortly after 2 o'clock on Thursday afternoon, January 6, and consisted of hearse, mourning coaches and railway officials from all over the country, numbering upwards of 60. The streets were thronged with hundreds of onlookers.

In the sobering aftermath of the funeral, the directors of the joint companies agreed to abide fully by the Act and have work on the new station intensified. In fact work of sorts had been in progress on the north side of Fishergate since 1872, the contractors being Messrs Banks, Thornton & Garside from Bolton. The work, however, was painfully slow, owing to legal implications relating to the purchase of property for demolition. It is recorded that Mr. Jabez. B. Jones, auctioneer, conducted a sale on August 8, 1872, of several houses and their contents on the north side of Fishergate, which had lately been occupied by a Mr. Sowerbutts, Mr. Harding and a number of tenants. Everything was sold on the day, including bricks, floorboards, slates, roof timbers, chimney pots, flagstones and household furniture from the demolished properties. Very little went to waste in those days. Work began on the demolition of the Fishergate tunnel in 1873, which again was found to be a slow and laborious task, involving much more time and expense than was originally estimated for. Inevitably, the firm had no other choice but to relinquish the contract owing to costs grossly exceeding estimates in every aspect of the work. After a protracted period of litigation, the contract was awarded to Cooper & Tullis of the Old Vicarage, Preston.

## Accident during construction of Fishergate bridge. 1877

In order to facilitate work on the Fishergate bridge, the contractors, Cooper & Tullis, took delivery of a steam crane from Smith & Sons, Rodley, near Leeds. By Friday, June 30, Mr. Smith and a team of engineers had assembled the crane and placed it on a 20 ft. length of track, which ran from the south end of the Victoria Hotel to a point, some 6 ft. beyond the buttress. It was conveniently placed for the purpose of hoisting excavated clay and debris from the foundation works, lifting the huge blocks of stone and lowering them into place. A large baulk of timber was chained athwart the rails at the buttress end. The crane was steamed and tested later on that day to the satisfaction of Mr. Smith, who succeeded in moving three tons of earth with the gauge showing 50 pounds per square inch. He then handed it over to one of the sub-contractors, Edward Bramley, a man with many years of experience in steam-powered machinery. The following morning, the crane was steamed again, and Mr. Bramley went round the motion with an oil can and turned steam on to warm the cylinders. He then cracked the regulator open in order to inject water into the boiler, but as he did so, the crane set off in the direction of the cutting. He was unable to stop it by closing the regulator and tried the reversing lever, which then sent the crane in the direction of the Victoria Hotel. He moved the lever to its original position, and this time the crane moved forward at a greater speed. Warnings were given and he managed to jump clear before it toppled over the buttress. Most of the men who had been working below managed to get out of the way, but two of the workmen, Michael Spencer and James Brennan lost their lives. Mr. Spencer was hit by the crane and died instantly, and Mr. Brennan was buried by the falling debris. It took some three hours to extricate him, and he was found to be severely scalded by the boiler water and steam. He died of his injuries shortly afterwards.

It would appear that there was too much steam pressure on at the time, and that Mr. Bramley had not thoroughly understood the instructions given him by Mr. Smith.

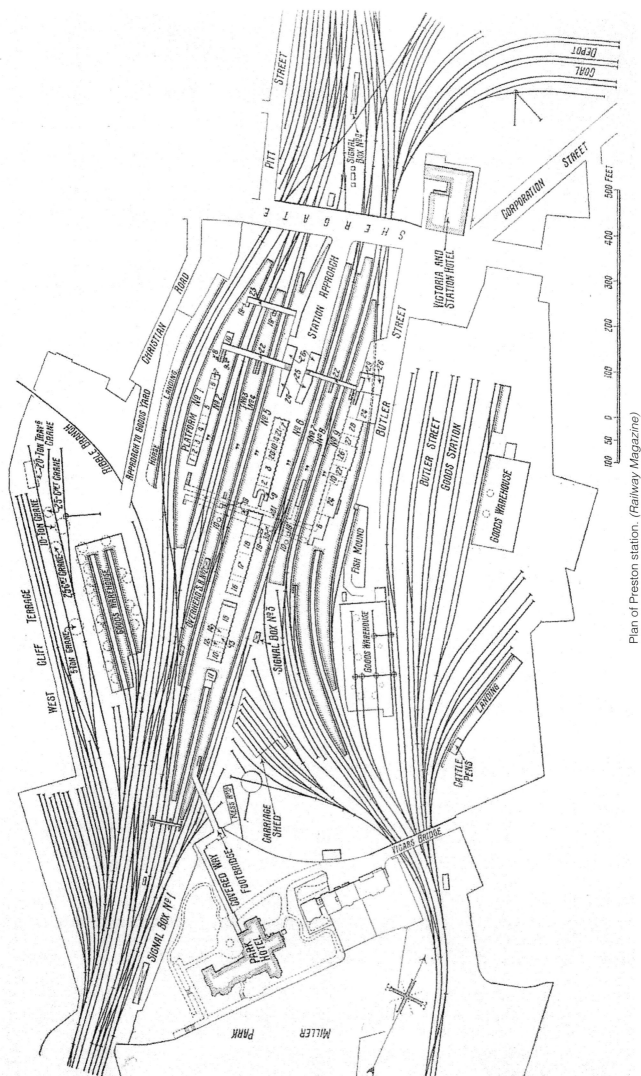

Plan of Preston station. (*Railway Magazine*)

**Plan of Preston Station key:**

1. Gentlemen's waiting room.
2. Ladies' first class waiting room.
3. Ladies' third class waiting room.
4. General waiting room.
5. Refreshment rooms.
6. Left luggage office.
7. Inspectors' office.
8. Tobacco stall.
9. Book stall.
10. Gentlemen's lavatories.
11. Carriage stores.
12. Telegraph office.
13. Re-booking office.
14. Ladies waiting room
15. Post Office room.
16. Refreshment room. Third class.
17. Refreshment room. First class.
18. Dining room.
19. Lift.
20. Gentlemen's waiting room. First class.
21. Stationmaster's office.
22. Footbridge.
23. Luggage bridge.
24. Parcel office.
25. Cloak room.
26. Booking office.
27. Waiting room,
28. Telegraph office, Stationmaster's office, guards and porters' rooms.
29. Booking hall.
30. Subway for luggage.
31. Subway for passengers.

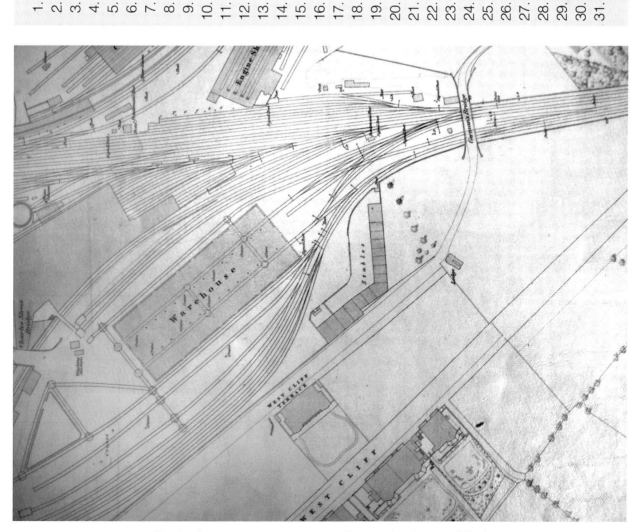

Charles Street goods, prior to 1879. *(Lancashire Records Office)*

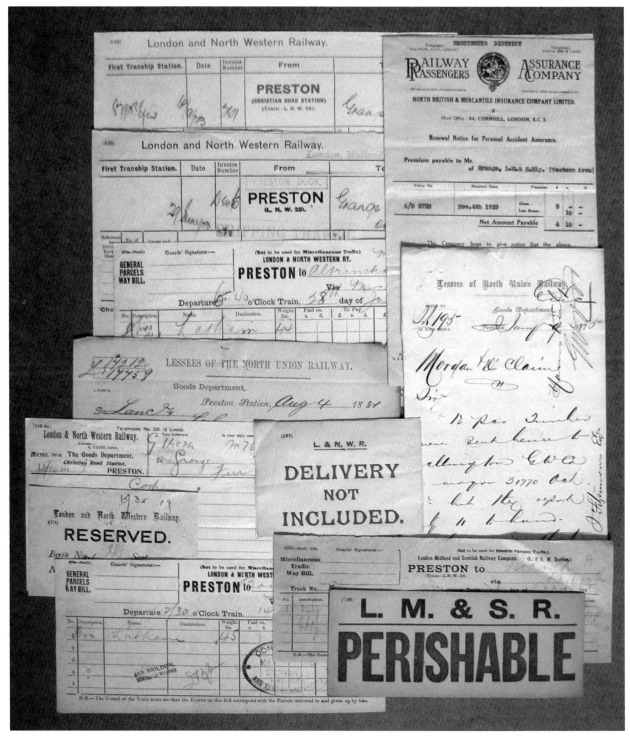

Documents, labels etc. pertaining to Preston station and goods. *(Author's collection)*

## Euxton Bridge, November 1877. Double collision

On Tuesday morning, 6th November, 1877, a double accident occurred at Euxton Junction, near the Black Saddle bridge, which crossed the road between Wigan and Preston. At 2.49 a.m., two goods trains were proceeding on their way to Preston; one from Manchester on the LYR route and the other from Wigan. The driver of the LNW engine, James Edwards, failed to notice the signal which was on at that moment, to allow the LYR train to pass through the junction, and continued without checking his speed. He was about 500 yards away from the signal box when he noticed the other train approaching the junction. He knew it was impossible to bring the train to a halt without fouling the junction points, so he opened the regulator full in the hope of clearing the points before the other train arrived; if this was to succeed, however, he would have had to rely on the judgement and skill of the signalman with regard to the point switches. He had got his train about half way across the points, when the collision occurred, and by an unaccountable piece of good fortune, the engine drivers, stokers and guards of both trains escaped without injury, although much havoc was played with the rolling stock. The tender of the LYR engine, the brake van and several trucks became detached and formed a heap of wreckage on the up line, while some of the wagons of the other train had been splintered by the impact, derailed and distributed over the rails on the down side of the embankment, which runs at an elevation of twenty feet from the level.

Before the bewildered railwaymen could realise what exactly had happened, a second collision took place. The Scotch night express had already passed on its way to Liverpool, but an hour later it was found necessary to run a relief express. This train had left Carlisle at 12 5 a.m., and comprised a fish and game van, a post office coach, two composite carriages, with first, second and third class compartments, and the guard's van. This train approached the scene of the accident at a speed of 60 miles an hour, with the driver having no idea of the obstacles which lay before him. But for the remarkable presence of mind of the pointsman, the ensuing collision would have been far more serious than it was. He switched the train over to the LYR siding, which he judged to be comparatively free of wreckage, but the tender and brake van from the LYR train had toppled over onto one of the rails. One can only imagine the terror and confusion amongst the passengers and crews in the pitch darkness. Assistance was called in from Preston, Chorley, Wigan and Manchester, and it was found that the express locomotive, although detached from its tender, had remained on the rails and had knocked the LYR tender, brake van and fish van down the embankment onto the road.

The post office coach had fallen over onto the side of the embankment and the two composite carriages had left the rails and were tottering dangerously on the edge of the narrow embankment. Notwithstanding the extent to which these two coaches had been damaged, not one of the passengers had received serious injuries.

The station master at Preston, Mr. Miles, hastened to the scene of the accident with an engine, brake van and single carriage. He was accompanied by Dr. Brown, the company's medical officer and a staff of assistants. On their arrival at Euxton, the passengers were examined, treated for minor injuries and, together with their luggage, placed in the vehicles which Mr. Miles had brought along with him. They were then taken to Preston and forwarded on from there to their respective destinations. Of the 34 passengers who had been travelling on the relief express, only 13 required treatment before continuing their journey. In the meantime, Mr. Worthington, the engineer, and Mr. Maddock, the Superintendent of the LYR Co., with Mr. Longbottom, Superintendent of the LNWR Locomotive Department at Preston, Mr. Purcell, District Superintendent at Lancaster, Inspector Cope and others, arrived at Euxton, and breakdown gangs from Preston and Wigan set to work clearing the line and repairing the track.

At the break of day, the usual crowds of spectators assembled in the vicinity of the junction to view the result of the catastrophe. The sight which met them resembled the aftermath of a battle: on both sides of the line, lying in confused masses were sacks of flour, fish, game, broken casks and crates; axles, wheels, pieces of broken iron and the shattered woodwork from wagons and carriages. At the time of the accident, work was in progress on widening the line to Preston, thus giving to the scene a more broken and desolating appearance. By mid-day, one line had been cleared, and some 4 hours later, all the tracks had been repaired and trains were running normally. It is conjectural that the debris of the LYR train fell upon the signal wires connecting the up line with the signal box, and in so doing, kept the signal in the off position for the relief express.

Hardly had the wreckage been removed from the lines at Euxton, when another incident occurred at Broughton station at around 4 o'clock that afternoon, when a heavily laden goods train travelling from London to Scotland was looped on the up line to make way for the Scotch express passenger train, which was due to leave Preston at 3 10 p.m. At the same time, another large goods train was travelling south on the up line, having left Lancaster at 3 50. As the train drew nearer, the driver leapt off the footplate and escaped unhurt. The collision which followed was of great force, and resulted in the engine and three wagons being knocked off the rails, blocking the down line. The accident was reported to Preston station just in time to prevent the Scotch express running into the wreckage. A wartime emergency situation arose, as superintendents Longbottom and Purcell selected a number of men from the Euxton breakdown gang and hastened north with jacks and levers to attend the scene at Broughton. Damaged wagons were unloaded and the contents placed in the cess until fresh wagons could be procured to take them on to their destinations. As darkness came on, bringing with it freezing cold temperatures and drizzling rain, fires and lanterns were lit. In the meantime, the Scotch express had come up within a safe distance of the scene, and some of the passengers alighted and strolled about muffled in their travelling coats, patiently and good-humouredly watching the progress of the work. At two minutes past nine, the down line was cleared and the train, which should have been in Scotland by that time, set off. The up line was cleared shortly after 10 o'clock. Notwithstanding the fact that there were fewer passengers killed or injured than railway servants, the travelling public came to regard the railway as a potential liability, especially during the hours of darkness. There were also the many instances of lost or damaged items of luggage and other personal belongings to take into consideration, the apprehension of which prompted many to seek out and obtain some form of travel insurance. The foremost in this line of business was the Railway Passenger's Assurance Company.[4]

In October 1876. the LNW introduced a new rule book with an additional clause forbidding the company's servants to enter a refreshment room for the purpose of drinking while on duty, on pain of dismissal. There were reasons for doing this, as the consumption of alcohol by railwaymen, both on and off the premises during working hours, was the cause of much concern to senior staff and passengers alike. It presented a bad image, and was considered by the management to have been the root cause of many mishaps, particularly where men were engaged upon the tracks. The company also tried to discourage passengers from tipping porters and guards, (engine drivers were also awarded handsome tips by businessmen to get them to their destinations on time) because extra coppers often meant extra refreshments, and once the 'Trinkgeld' had been placed in their hands, they were off to the alehouse for a jar or two.

L.N.W.R. official postcard, looking north along platform 5. There's plenty of detail to absorb here, including the 'bird-cage' brake, tobacconist's kiosk, pigeon baskets and an indicator board for the Park Station Hotel. *(Author's collection)*

## Demolition of Skew Bridge, Sunday, March 3, 1878

On Sunday morning, March 3, 1878, the skew bridge on Leyland Road, Penwortham was demolished as part of the track widening work between Preston and Euxton. Some 2,000 people gathered in the immediate vicinity to watch the operation. Several charges of dynamite were placed just below the spring line of the stone arch, and fired successfully with the greater part of the arch collapsing on the timber crash-deck which protected the rails below. Some 50 or so workmen moved in with picks and demolished the remaining blocks of masonry. A locomotive and steam crane were then brought in to remove the rubble, and within an hour, the up line was cleared. The bulk of the debris had fallen across the down line, and it was 4 30 in the afternoon before the line was cleared. A temporary wooden structure had been erected within a few yards of the old bridge.

Postcard, looking south along platform 5 in L.N.W.R days.

## Opening of Preston new station Sunday, September 21, 1879

Work on the station progressed satisfactorily, with the main island platform being opened for traffic on the morning of Sunday, September 21, 1879. A staff of 150 men arrived at the station around 06.00 and commenced setting up points and signals etc. The first trains to arrive were those from Fleetwood and Lancaster on the east side of the platform; later on, at 2.40 in the afternoon, a train left the west platform for Blackpool and the 5 and 6 o'clock, trains set off from the east platform for Manchester and Liverpool. Tickets were issued at the main entrance for all trains except those on the East Lancashire section. The old booking, parcels and left-luggage offices on Butler Street were closed following the departure of the 08.30 train to Wigan and Liverpool. The station was still a long way off completion, and the London trains were still running from the old Charles Street station. Of particular interest was the erection of two large, double-faced cantilever clocks on either side of the main buildings, by Mr. Joyce of Whitchurch. The principle superintendents and traffic managers of the line were present: Mr. Purcell and Mr. Turnbull of Lancaster, Mr. Thompson of Crewe, Mr. G.J.Crosbie Dawson, engineer, Mr. Miles, Station Master and Mr. Illingworth of the booking department. There was no ceremony as such; the opening was of a formal character, with a large number of people visiting the station between the opening time and 10.50 pm; the general opinion amongst most of them was that the building was more commodious and imposing than they could have imagined. The visitors were particularly impressed by the size of the public rooms and the height of the ceilings. The furniture within was supplied by the firm of Bell and Coupland of Preston, and Gillows of Lancaster, the plumbing, boilers etc. having been supplied by Benthams of London. The general waiting room was fitted out with solid oak tables and chairs and the floor was covered with corticine.[5]

The gentlemen's first class waiting room was furnished with upholstered oak chairs, and the ladies' first class rooms had mahogany seats covered in Morocco leather; there were also two luxurious arm chairs covered in the same material and three side tables. The ladies' second and third class rooms were fitted up in the same manner as the general room. The centre block on the main platform contained the main dining room, which was 64 ft in length by 30ft.; and two refreshment rooms, each being 50ft by 30ft.; all three rooms were superbly furnished. Cooper & Tullis subcontracted all the plumbing, glazing and painting work to Messrs. Wilding of Lune Street, Preston. The length of the main platform was 1,225 ft. with a width of 110 ft. Two subways, one for passengers and the other for luggage and parcels, were constructed at the south end, with passages branching off to storage rooms; added to these were the numerous ducts for service pipes and cables etc.

The eastern island was opened on Sunday, July 18, 1880, following the completion of track work and new signalling. A Board of Trade inspector, the signalling superintendent, Mr. Dick, and the resident engineer, Mr. Crosbie Dawson were in attendance. A new entrance for the L.Y.R. with waiting rooms, offices etc. was completed on the Butler Street side at the same time. On the west side, the Charles

Street building was still standing, albeit half derelict, and work was still going on with the erection of the new roof. There were still only two lines north of Fishergate Bridge, which formed a bottleneck; this was partly remedied when work commenced in August 1880 on two up and two down lines and a fifth line for the engine shed. The width of the Fishergate bridge was built in two, 30 ft. sections, and was opened in 1879. The original plans for the approach to the main island platform included a flight of 35 stone steps, with a hoist for luggage and parcels etc. The town council was not in favour of this and wanted the booking office and entrance to be on a level with the platforms. Space was at a premium then, as it is now, and it was eventually agreed to connect the booking office with the platform by means of a ramp. In the light of the fact that the main entrance was some 7 ft. higher than the platform, and a distance of 110 yards from the nearest station building, it was suggested that a booking office be opened on the platform and horse-drawn carriages be permitted to run directly to it from Fishergate.

Looking south along platform 6. Note the LNW. signals, and trolley with carriage-ends. *(H.C. Casserley)*

## New gas lamp for station, 1879

One of the new Sugg pattern lamps was erected close to the entrance of the station by the gas company, on behalf of the Corporation.[6] This was a 200 candle burner and was equal in brilliance to 12 of the ordinary gas lights. Two similar lamps were located in front of the gas company's offices in Fishergate, these being 8 candle burners, equal to 5 of the ordinary lamps. They were similar in design to those in Waterloo Road, London, and were the focus of much interest when they were lit for the first time on Christmas Eve, 1879. Although a little more expensive than the conventional type, they were deemed, if generally adopted, to be of great benefit to the town. The station itself was illuminated by the pendant lantern type gas lamps, of the Sugg 'Westminster' pattern. On the subject of gas lighting, it was some two years later, in 1881, that the L.N.W. decided to follow the example of the L.Y.R. by installing gas lights in their carriages, the dim, dirty and often dangerous oil lamps having been subject to much criticism from the travelling public over the years.

Following the demolition of the dilapidated temporary structures at Charles Street, the station was extended further westwards, and by 1903, the number of platforms had increased to nine. Beginning at the west side, the first platform as such was the 'horse dock', which was also for the transshipment of other livestock and circus animals; then came the first island island platform, with No. 1 being used as the main down platform for Blackpool traffic, and No. 2, which was signalled for both up and down traffic, but used mainly for up trains from Blackpool to Liverpool or Manchester. This platform was also used for trains

There's a whole wealth of fascinating detail in this picture, showing the wreckage of the 'Scotch Express', which ran off the tracks just to the north of the station in July, 1896. The train was double-headed by 2-4-0 locomotives, 275 Vulcan and 2159 Shark. They were travelling at 40 miles per hour instead of the regulatory 10. (*Harris Museum*)

## L.M. & S.R.—Carriage & Wagon Department.

C. F. 194.
5/25.

Scott     Hy     BORN   27. 7. 92

STATIONED AT _____ Preston

OCCUPATION _____ Washer.

| DATE. | OCCUPATION, PROMOTIONS, REMOVALS, REDUCTIONS, AND PUNISHMENTS. | Rate of WAGES. | WAR WAGE or BONUS. |
|---|---|---|---|
| | Entered Service as *May 1912.* | | |
| | Transferred from Colne | | |
| 15 1 26 | to Gasmakers Asst. vice J Wignall | 48/- | 3/- |
| 11 10 26 | " Washer own request | | |
| 19 9 27 | to Gasfitter vice Kirkland | | |
| 6 8 28 | ' Washer. Economics & Kirkham | | |
| 25 8 28 | Gas Filler Vice Kirkland | 46/- | 2/- |
| 16-7-37 | Basic rate advance Barnes Wir SW 520/3 2-9-37 | 43/- | 1/- |
| 1 4 31 | Cost of Living Rate 1/4/31 | 45/- | |
| 5 12 32 | Transferred to Fleetwood as Cleaner vice Davitt | 42/- | |
| 9 9 33 | { Promoted to Chg hand vice R Billington transferred to London | 46/- | |
| ~~29 10 33~~ | ~~Advance Mr xxxxxxxxxxxxxx 17 2 40~~ | ~~56/-~~ | ~~58/-~~ |
| 20 11 35 | Reverted to Car Cleaner at Own Request | 42/- | |
| 27 1 36 | Transferred as Greaser to Lostock Hall vice Butcher (Self discharged) | 42/- | |
| 1 1 37 | Cost of Living Bonus recommenced | 42/- | 1/- |
| 16 8 37 | Basic Rate advanced 1/- Auth. 520/3 of 4/4 | 43/- | 1/- |
| 1 10 37 | { Cost of Living Bonus advanced 1/- Authority S.W. 94/14 of 5/10/37 | 43/- | 2/- |
| 1 1 38 | { Cost of Living Bonus advanced 1/- Authority SW 94/14 of 31 Dec/37 | 43/- | 3/- |
| 14 3 38 | Transferred to Lostock Hall Wgn Shop at Temp. Lifter for Training Authority SW 4427/91 | 32/- 0/9 | 16/6 3/38 |
| 2 5 38 | Transferred to Preston for relief Car. exam training | | |
| 4 7 38 | Temporary Lifter at Wyre Dock, vice O. Ref, Reclassified Authority SW 4936/28 | 32/- | 16/6 |

LMSR employment card for Henry Scott, born July 1892 and commenced work in May 1912. He spent most of his working life in the Preston area. *(Authors Collection)*

*Ilott H.*

| DATE. | OCCUPATION, PROMOTIONS, REMOVALS, REDUCTIONS, AND PUNISHMENTS. | Rate of WAGES. | WAR WAGE or BONUS. |
|---|---|---|---|
| 18 7 38 | Transferred to Wyre Dock, as Brake Adjuster Authority. Mr Barnes. S.W. 81/12. of 13/7/38 | 56/- | |
| 29-10-39 | Advance Mr. Staniers letter 17-2-40 | 56/- | 58/- |
| 1-1-40 | " " " " | 58/- | 4/- WW |
| 3-6-40 | Stanier 11-6-40 C.O. L. | 58/- | |
| 6 1 41 | do 20/5/41 do | 58/- | 4/- |
| 9-3-42 | Advance Staniers SW 520/16- 20-5-42 | 58/- | 13-6 |
| 24-6-42 | Advance Fairburn SW520/18- 17-12-42. | 58/- | 18/6 |
| 26 4 43 | " " " " /19. 26.6.43. | 58/- | 23/- |
| 14 4 44 | " " " /22 25.4.44 | " | 28/- |
| 30-7-45 | Advance SW 520/26- 27-8-45 | 94/6 | |
| 29 9 46 | Transferred to Farington Carriage Shed as Examiner, New appointment. SR,4936/1903. | 3/3/46.94/6 | |
| 13/8/47. | Transferred to Preston as Carriage Cleaner, own request. see P.File. | 92/6. | |
| 27.6.49 | *to Operating Dept* | | |

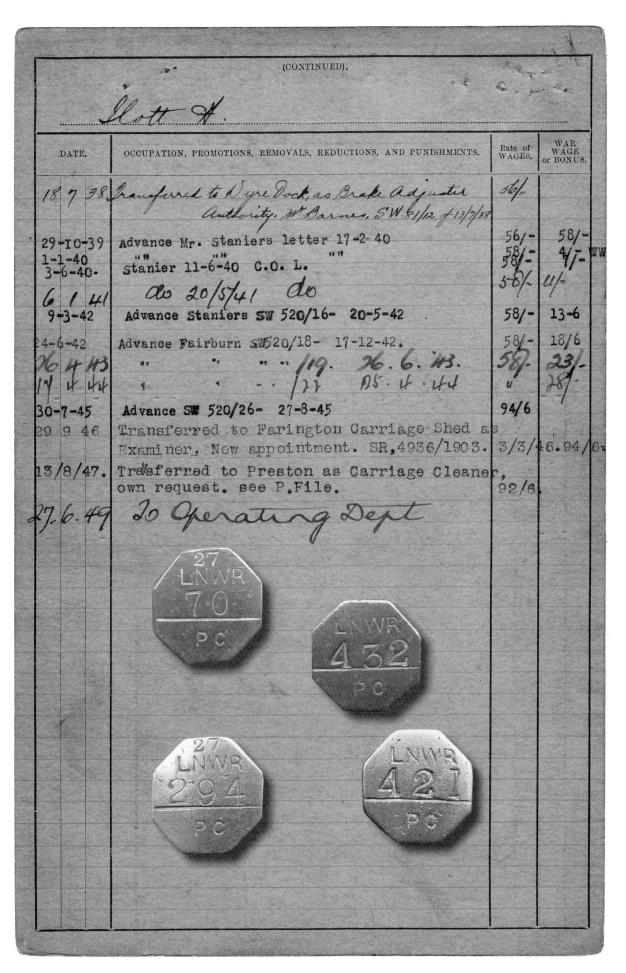

Reverse side of employment card together with four brass pay-tokens as used by Preston railway servants. The number 27 denotes the engine shed. *(Authors Collection)*

working the Longridge branch. A centre track was built between platforms 3 and 4 with cross-overs for the transfer of stock and engine movements; it was also used for the temporary storage of empty passenger stock. The island platforms, 3 and 4 were comparatively narrow with no facilities such as waiting rooms etc. and were used mainly for local stopping trains. No. 3 was signalled for two-way traffic and No. 4 was used as a loop for No. 5, with cross-overs between both platform faces for the transfer of stock and engine movements. Numbers 5 and 6 constituted the main island platforms; No. 5 being the down fast to Carlisle and Scotland and No. 6 the up fast to Birmingham and London. As mentioned earlier, the main station entrance and facilities were located between these platforms, which also had two bays at the south end, numbers 5A and 6A. The island platforms, 7 and 8 were narrow and shorter than those previously mentioned, with no buildings. No. 7 was served by a loop line which served the same purpose for No. 6, as No. 4 did for No. 5, and No. 8 was the L.&Y. Railway's down platform on the East Lancashire section. No. 9 platform served the up traffic for the same company and was part of a complete station in itself, with booking office, waiting rooms etc. which had its own entrance on Butler Street.[7]

In 1882, a glazed and roofed iron bridge was built from the end of the main island platform to an elegant reception building on the west side of the Cliff. From here, railway travellers could reach the newly opened Station Hotel by way of a glazed and roofed corridor.[8] The construction of the Park Hotel, as it became known, was a joint venture between the L.N.W. and L & Y companies. It is a magnificent building and still dominates the south-east end of the station. It ceased to function as an hotel in 1950 when the building was sold to Lancashire County Council for use as offices. The 'Glass Bridge' as it was referred to by a generation of railway enthusiasts, remained in use for the convenience of L.C.C. staff and visitors to the offices travelling to Preston by rail. The 1972 electrification plans included a proposal to either drop the bridge (which carried the number 122), or have it raised to a higher level, in order to meet the minimum height for clearance. The cost of raising it was too great, and the bridge was removed in June of that year.

Fowler class 7F 0-8-0, 49508 from Newton Heath shed, approaches platform 9 with a train of empty mineral wagons on September 2, 1952. *(Frank Dean)*

C.T. Notice No. 182 G.

# L. & N. W. Rly.

## NOTICE OF

### SPECIAL TRAIN AND OTHER ARRANGEMENTS

#### IN CONNECTION WITH THE

# PRESTON GUILD

## September 4th to 9th, inclusive.

# ROYAL
# Lancashire Agricultural Show

## AT PRESTON.

### SEPTEMBER 6th, 7th, 8th, and 9th.

A **Stand-by Train** to be at Preston (Farington Slow Line Sidings) from September 4 to 9, inclusive.

### STRENGTHENING AND RELIEF, ETC., ARRANGEMENTS.

| Dates. Sept. | Train. | Extra Vehicles and Relief Arrangements. |
|---|---|---|
| 4 to 9 | 6.45 a.m., Wigan to Oxenholme | 2 thirds. |
| 4 to 9 | 6.15 a.m., Crewe to Preston | 2 thirds. |
| 4 to 9 | 8.15 a.m., Liverpool to Morecambe | 2 thirds. |
| 4 to 9 | 11.20 a.m., Preston to Windermere | To start from Wigan at 10.39 a.m. as an excursion, and arrive Preston 11.10 a.m. See page 4. |
| 4 to 9 | 11.45 a.m., Wigan to Morecambe | Liverpool strengthening set. |
| 9 | 1.50 p.m., Preston to Morecambe | To be formed of Division " B " set usually on 3.0 p.m. from Preston. |
| 8 | 9.20 a.m. season excursion, Euston to Carlisle | Will not convey a portion for Blackpool. |
| 4 to 9 | 3.27 p.m., Preston to Carlisle | The Liverpool and Manchester to Windermere vehicles to leave Preston at 3.18 p.m. See page 5. |

1

Train arrangements for 1922 Guild. *(Author's collection)*

James Bagshaw (on the right) was a wheel-tapper at the station for many years.
He is seen here with his mates at the Butler Street workshops. *(Courtesy, Jason Bagshaw)*

LMS wheel-tapper's hammer as used by James Bagshaw. *(Author)*

In order to facilitate the movement of exhibits for the Royal Agricultural Society's show at Moor Park, which opened on July 15, 1885, the L.N.W. obligingly laid down a temporary track from the cattle market siding at Oxheys to the site of the show ground, from where it branched out in a number of sidings. A sleeper platform, 160 ft. long by 18 ft. wide, was erected for the debarkation of animals and farming implements, and a steam crane was supplied to lift the heavier items of machinery such as traction engines etc. out of the railway trucks. A temporary stable for the railway horses was built, together with cook houses and other conveniences for the men. The work was carried out by Mr. Creighton, the railway engineer and Mr. John Yates, the permanent way inspector for the L.N.W. and L & Y railways. Altogether, 438 horses, 589 cattle, 433 sheep, 203 pigs, 1165 birds were transported together with numerous items of machinery and steam engines. Once all the agricultural material had been delivered, the platform was rearranged, cleaned up and decorated in readiness for the arrival of the Prince of Wales on June 16. The following day he was taken to the site of the new docks where he laid a foundation stone.[9]

1914 – 1918 railway service badge.

Free buffet cloth badge.

All: *(Mike Atherton Collection)*

Perhaps one of the more notable events at the station occurred on August 19th, 1915, when a free buffet for servicemen was opened. It was the concept of a group of benevolent local ladies, led by a Mrs. Moore, who realised that the growing numbers of sailors and soldiers in transit would require food, drink and shelter during the long intervals between trains. They formed a committee and approached the L.N.W.R. who kindly provided them with a room on the main island platform, to the south of the main subway. The location was ideal, as most of the naval and troop trains arrived and departed from these platforms. The buffet was open 24 hours a day and was staffed by over 300 volunteers; it proved to be a great success and soon made a name for itself, thanks to the energy and organisational skills of Mrs. Moore, who acted as Hon. Treasurer and Manageress. Unfortunately she was compelled to stand down some 12 months later; the incessant hard work and commitment having taken its toll. On the opening day, 386 men were served, and in the week before Christmas 1916, 12,449 men were served in 36 hours. The average number of men served in January 1917 was calculated at 3,250 men in every 24 hour period. Makeshift beds were made out of benches; newspapers and magazines were issued and writing materials provided for those precious letters home. Messages of appreciation and donations in the form of cash, foodstuffs, blankets etc. poured in from the public and servicemen alike; a flag day was held on November 25th, 1916, and raised over £320 for the buffet. The otherwise parsimonious Admirals of the Grand Fleet made an exception and donated a quantity of flags, which helped to raise £4. The expenditure at the beginning was around £30 per week, and had risen to £100 per week by 1917. Tea, coffee, cocoa, buns and biscuits were provided free, and sandwiches, meat pies, tobacco and cigarettes were charged for at cost price or less. As an act of appreciation for all the assistance that had been given them by the stationmaster and his staff, the volunteers subscribed to a hot-pot supper, which was given to all the staff over a period of two days. By the end of the war, the remarkable and tireless ladies of Preston had served more than three million cups of tea and other refreshments. A similar arrangement was made at the station in the same room during the course of the second global débâcle in 1939, whereby another generation of like-minded ladies served over eight million travelling servicemen and women with free refreshments.[10]

Officers and Executive Committee for the free buffet, 1916/17. Standing (from the left),
Mrs. Blackhurst, Mrs. Bell, Mrs. Foster, Mrs. Threlfall. Seated, Mrs. Woodcock,
the Mayoress (Mrs. Cartmell), Mrs. Todd, Mrs. Eastwood. *(Lancashire Evening Post)*

Buns and brews all round during another busy wartime day at the station.
*(Lancashire Evening Post)*

## James Byrns

On Thursday, November 14, 1889, a long serving and highly respected railwayman, James Byrns, died at his home in Haugh, near Bolton. He retired from the railway in March, 1868, after serving 22 years as station master at Preston. He was born in Kent in the year 1799 and grew up to personify one of those few links which connected the old fashioned methods of travelling and communication with those of the late 19th century. He saw the old stage coaches in their heyday, when people were content to travel between London and Edinburgh in a week and receive news at a correspondingly slow rate. He witnessed the revolution created by the introduction of steam and electricity; and briefly, he practically linked the past with the present in the above respect most completely, and constituted a person unique in his line and very rarely met with. In his early days he was guard of the mail coach between Manston and Derby, via Matlock, then moved north and became guard of the coach which ran between Lancaster and Carlisle, via Shap Fells. This was mainly night work, with the coach leaving Lancaster at 9 p.m. and returning from Carlisle at 7 p.m. the next night. Subsequently, when the railway reached Carlisle, the coaches fell into disuse, and Mr. Byrns obtained the appointment of station master at Preston, succeeding an Irishman by the name of Etterick in 1846. During his time in office, the able manner in which he discharged his duties, and the courteous and cheerful disposition which he invariably displayed towards all with whom he came into contact, won for him the utmost respect of those who laboured under his judicious, but not exacting, charge, and the great esteem of innumerable passengers north and south. Mr. Byrne possessed a capital fund of anecdotes and could spin stories of his own experiences in the old coaching days; hence, in company he was highly entertaining. During the course of an interview with the famous Preston Historian, Hewitson, he recollected the time when he put the wife of an inflated official, connected with the Lancaster & Preston Railway, in the first class carriage of a north-bound train. Two days later, he received a letter from the lady asking him what he had been thinking about, as the train journey had been a particularly unpleasant one, and that her teeth had been all but shaken out of her mouth. The fault rested with neither the station master nor the carriage, but with the condition of the track, which had been made from an inferior quality iron, and the the stone blocks upon which they were laid.[11]

L.N.W. 4-6-0 No. 2275, at the north end of platform 5, circa 1914. *(H. Gordon Tidy)*

On Tuesday, November 11, 1856, he received a testimonial in recognition of his eleven years as superintendent of the station. The testimonial comprised a service of silver plate to the value of £65, and a very handsome purse containing £150. The inscription on the coffee pot stated the sum of money to have been 120 Guineas, but after the plate was purchased and the inscription engraved, more subscriptions came in, and the amount was raised to £150. The plate was supplied by Mr. Hall of Manchester. A most excellent supper was served up at the Bull Hotel assembly rooms, which was attended by between 60 and 70 of the 300 or so subscribers. The chairman, Mr. E. Pedder, complemented Mr. Byrnes on his outstanding ability to manage the day to day affairs at a station which was wholly unsuitable for the demands made upon it. The chairman recalled an occasion when Mr. Byrnes risked his life to rescue a lady who had been in great danger upon the tracks (cheering), and her husband's indignant remark about wanting to know what right he had to touch her (laughter). "That person," continued the chairman, "must have been rather anxious to get rid of his wife." (laughter). Mr. Byrnes mentioned that he never took particular care of the rich and never neglected the poor. He once found a very young waif of a lad on the station who was totally confused as to which train he should have been travelling on. On questioning the lad, Mr. Byrnes discovered that he hadn't enough money on him to pay for the full fare. Not only did he make up the cost of the ticket out of his own pocket, he also took the lad over to the refreshment room and treated him to a much needed square meal. There followed many more speeches and toasts, including a word or two of gratitude for Mrs. and Miss Lambert, and Mrs. Irving, who worked in the refreshment rooms, for the disinterest and substantial kindness they had invariably shown to the returning soldiers of the Crimean campaign when passing through the station; and to widows and orphans of others. He had seen these people arrive at Preston station with drooping hearts and sorrowful countenances, and had seen them depart with pleasure-beaming eyes, and with blessings on their lips for those worthy women, who had furnished them with refreshments and put money in their pockets to cover the costs of their journey home (long and loud applause). He concluded his speech with a reading of the inscription on the plate:

*To Mr. James Byrnes,*
*Superintendent of the Railway Station, Preston.*
*This Testimonial,*
*Consisting of silver tea and coffee service, and its*
*appendages, together with*
*a Purse of 120 Guineas,*
*Is presented by a large body of friends, as a memento of their*
*esteem for his character, and of their high sense of the courtesy,*
*assiduity and skill with which he has, for upwards of 11 years,*
*managed the complicated business committed to his charge.*
*Preston, Nov. 11th, 1856.*

On his retirement in 1868, he was succeeded by Mr. Lomax, who for many years had been senior inspector at the station; his place, in turn, had been taken by Mr. Eckersley; PC Draper was promoted to Mr. Eckersley's former position and PC Ingham was promoted from second to first station policeman. Non of the above-mentioned officers received a commensurate increase in salary. The out-going station master fared no better, as his only reward for so many years of hard and loyal service was a vote of thanks from the board of directors. He landed on his feet (albeit for a brief spell), when he became the proprietor of the Bull & Royal Hotel in Preston, after marrying the incumbent proprietress, Mrs. Townsend.[12] He was not long there, however, and moved to Cottam where he resided until 1885, when he moved again to live with his daughter in Manchester. They had only been there a few months, when she was taken ill and died and, subsequently, the house was vacated and Mr. Byrns went to live with a grandson in Bolton. His duration there was brief, and he took an apartment in Bury New Road, Haugh, near Bolton, where he died at the age of 90. The following Monday his remains were interred in a vault at Brooklands, near Manchester, where he was reunited with his daughter.

The ill-fated Britannia Pacific, 70017 Arrow, is about to depart from platform 5 on April 21, 1965. Note the parcels van in the 'Derby' bay on the left. *(Tony Gillett)*

Aerial photo of the Fishergate end of the station, circa 1920. *(British Railways Board)*

The new station was well able to cope with the increasing number of passengers at ordinary times, but when it came to holidays and other extraordinary occasions, staff were called in from the less busy stations in the area to help out. A form of crowd control had to be implemented, whereby only so many people were allowed to be on the narrower platforms at any one time, and officers had to be on hand to keep people clear of the platform edges. The L.Y. R. had worked this method to a fine art, and had published a booklet on their achievements at Blackpool North station. People were literally herded like cattle from the concourses to the platforms and vice versa by way of narrow, open gangways and barrier gates. This wasn't entirely the case at Preston, but similar measures were put in place, using officers as human walls and barriers. Passenger numbers for the Easter weekend of 1890 are recorded as being particularly high, with 200 booked for Windermere and about 300 to Morecambe on Good Friday morning. 500 were booked for the full day trip to Blackpool in the morning, and some 700 in the afternoon; the East Lancs. side sent 100 to Southport and 120 to Liverpool , and the West Lancs. station conveyed about 500 to Southport. On Easter Monday, another 250 booked for Morecambe, and day tickets to Blackpool numbered 1,100, with 2,000 booking half-day tickets. All these passengers were conveyed on special trains. Altogether, during the entire weekend, around 10,000 people travelled to various seaside resorts from Preston; and that on Good Friday alone, the three companies carried a total of 25,750 people to Blackpool from Liverpool, Manchester, Wigan, East Lancashire and West Yorkshire via Preston. These numbers were to grow progressively throughout the following decades and remained high in the years leading up to the mid 1960's. The West Lancashire Railway had been opened in time to take some of the weight off the central station during the Merchant Guild of 1882; such was the density of traffic, however, that part of the goods warehouse at Charles Street had to be adapted to handle passenger traffic. By the time of the grouping in 1923, the staff at Preston comprised one station master, 3 assistant station masters, 9 platform inspectors, 3 main line inspectors, 5 station foremen, 5 yard foremen, 2 parcels foremen, 59 signalmen, 4 relief signalmen and 14 signal boys (train-

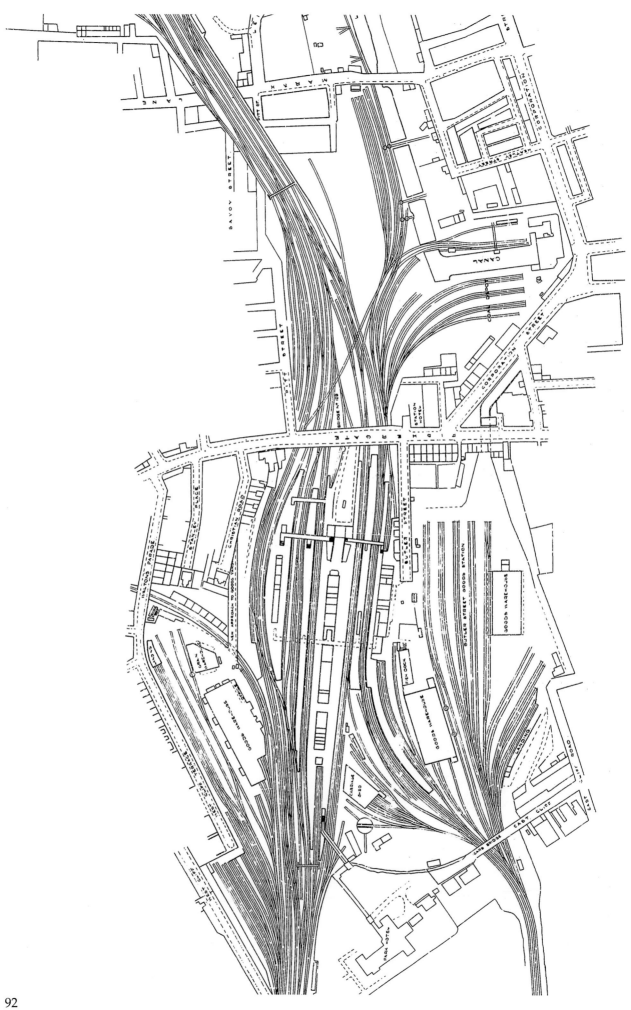

92

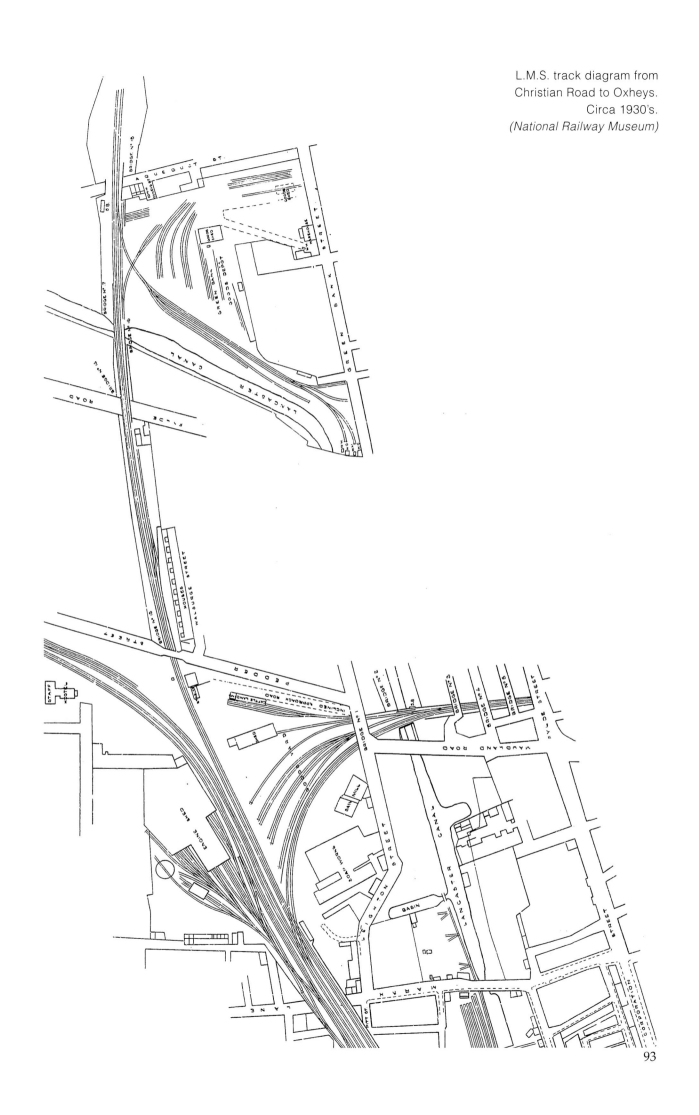

L.M.S. track diagram from
Christian Road to Oxheys.
Circa 1930's.
*(National Railway Museum)*

bookers); 87 ordinary and parcels porters, 10 train reporters, 25 foremen and ordinary ticket collectors, 4 train attendants, 29 guards, 22 shunters, 11 cloakroom and waiting room attendants; a chief clerk, a staff clerk, 3 ordinary clerks and 2 enquiry office clerks. These numbers would have been increased during the Summer month

Jubilee, 45574, India, ready for the off at platform 5 on October 15, 1964. *(Tony Gillett)*

Jubilee, 45561, Saskatchewan, emerges from the shadows on Platform 9, on March 3, 1962. *(Tony Gillett)*

The station master in 1952 was Mr. R.G. Ellis, who carried on with the time honoured tradition of wearing a top hat and frock coat. On a visit from the reporter of the British Railways Magazine in that year, he proudly showed him the drop-case fusee driven wall clock, with the legend 'N.U. No. 6' on the dial, which dated from 1838. There was also a brass handbell with L.N.W.R. in relief letters. This was one of two bells which were used to notify passengers in the refreshment rooms on platforms 5 and 6 that the Anglo-Scottish trains were about to depart. From 1863 onwards, the up and down expresses used to arrive at Preston around the same time, and the passengers had just 20 minutes to partake of refreshments before the trains departed. The second bell, marked L&YR, is alleged to have been borrowed by a consortium of North End football fans, for the purpose of injecting some voltage into the players. It was a predictably futile gesture, as the voltage went the other way, and worse still, the bell was never returned. I would dearly like to know what fate befell these irreplaceable railway artefacts. Mr. Ellis superseded Joseph Hood, who had begun his career with the L.Y.R. In 1893, and had held the post of station master since the memorable year of 1923. Prior to his appointment at Preston, Mr. Hood had served as goods clerk at Blackpool Talbot Road; then station master at Wrea Green in 1900; station master at Salwick in 1904; the same post including that of clerk in charge at Lytham in 1908; station master at Blackpool, Waterloo Road in 1912 and the same post at Blackpool Talbot Road in 1917. Bob Tye said of him, "He lived in the Fylde area, and would arrive at Preston each day around 9 o'clock. He was a meticulously smart man, and always concerned about the cleanliness of the station. He would don a pair of white gloves and stroll about the main platforms, running his hands here and there on a window sill or the back of a bench in the waiting room, and if he discovered any undesirable marks on those gloves, he would upbraid the person responsible for keeping that particular part of the building clean. He would give that person just one sharp warning, and if it happened a second time, he would be suspended from duty for a couple of days without pay. We had a nice clean station in those days."

Mr. Ellis was superseded by Mr. Hazeldene, who was the last man to hold the position of station master as such, and differed from his predecessors in that he wore a derby or bowler hat instead of the traditional top hat. Following his departure in the early 1970's, the title was changed to 'station manager.'

The driver of 71000, Duke of Gloucester, is taking advantage of the light at the south end, in order to read his instructions, on June 6, 1961. The 'DOG', as she was known, gave a better account of herself following restoration and preservation than she ever did in B.R. Days. *(Tony Gillett)*

A fireman's view of the north end of the Ribble bridge, from the footplate of a Fowler class 4 tank.
The engine in the lead is a Metrovic type 2 Co Bo, with a Birmingham R. C. & W. DMU
in second place. *(Tony Gillett)*

A considerable amount of modification work was carried out at the north end in 1960-63, which involved cutting back the station roof, the removal of the 'parcels' footbridge and the replacement of semaphore signals with aspect lights. The administration offices on the station were vacated in 1966, following the completion of a new office building at Ladywell Street. Ladywell House, as it became known, was built on the site of the canal wharf, the actual basin itself having been filled in to make way for a staff car park (the offices were closed and most of the remaining staff transferred to Crewe in the 1990's). Staff wages continued to be paid out at Butler Street, and rooms on the former L&Y platform 9 were used by the area medical officer, mainly for eyesight tests on footplate crews and signalmen.

Station pilot, 46762, a former Wirral Railway loco, banks a heavy freight up
the gradient to Maudland on April 21, 1951. *(H.C. Casserley)*

Perhaps the most memorable occasion within living memory at the station took place on the evening of August 3, 1968, when Lostock Hall Black 5, 45318 (driver, Ernie Heyes and fireman, Tony Smith) departed with the 9.25 for Liverpool Exchange. This was to be the last officially scheduled, steam hauled passenger train to leave Preston (and the last train as such on the entire B.R. Standard gauge system), some 130 years after the arrival of the North Union Railway. The penultimate steam hauled train left the station at 8.50 that same evening with a train to Blackpool South. The engine was another Black 5, 45212, from the same stable, with driver Bob Barker and fireman, Mel Rigby. For the remainder of the evening and into the following day, this engine worked as Preston station pilot, thus becoming the very last steam loco to carry out normal duties for British Railways. Other memorable 'last ones' to be played out in the 60's included the Southport – Preston passenger service, on September 6, 1964, and the steam-hauled Belfast Boat Express (Manchester Victoria – Heysham), on February 29, 1968. This service was withdrawn altogether in 1975. A familiar voice at the station in the 1960's was that of Mrs. Irene Sergeant, and it is only recently that I have had the pleasure of putting a name to that voice, which came over the P.A. system and was difficult to make out above the reverberating sounds of a busy station. A local newspaper referred to her as being 'the new train jockey,' and she was there on that historical evening to announce the departure of the final steam hauled service trains.

*"Back in those days we had piped music and I interrupted this to make announcements. Robert Oliver was in charge then, and I remember attending for an interview at Ladywell House. I was shown into a little room and placed in front of a microphone, where I was asked to read prose from a sheet of paper, while the senior officials listened in another room. I can remember getting a mention on Radio Caroline. They were in the process of being closed down at the time, so they referred to the music and me on the station and how unfair it was to allow this but not theirs."*

Black 5, 45046, in distress beneath the 'Glass Bridge', on May 12, 1965. The driver and Mr. Sedgebeer, the Lostock Hall Shed master, examine the front driver which has ended up on the floor.
Mr. Sedgebeer's breakdown train, to which he was particularly attached, was waiting alongside the Preston No. 1 box. *(Tony Gillett)*

The 1950's were by far the best years for train-watching at Preston (and just about everywhere else in the country for that matter); unfortunately, I can only remember the last three years of that decade, and by the time I was old enough to be turned loose on the world in the early 60's, many of the pre-groupers and 'namers' had gone. Here, therefore, is an account of what was to be seen from the line-side in those golden years and the following decade of decline by Ben Brooksbank.[13]

*"It was almost impossible to see every train at once on Preston station, and I was aware of missing a few trains as they passed each other on the main lines, and as they crept round on the East Lancashire lines. On the other hand, trains to and from Scotland, the North-East and Blackpool passed through twice, using the Preston Junction and Farington curves. On July 27th, 1950, I was on the station from 12.45 to 17.30 and noted 170 locomotive workings (11 twice), individually comprising 9 Pacifics, 5 Royal Scots, 9 Patriots, 11 Jubilees, 53 Black 5's (five twice); 4 x 4-4-0's, 18 x 2-6-0's, 16 of which were 'Crabs' (3 twice); 15 x 0-6-0's, all on passenger work, with 3 being ex-LYR , one piloting a Jubilee; 15 x 2-6-4 tanks (5 twice); 3 x 2-6-2, 3 x 2-4-2 and 2 x 0-6-0 tanks; also the two Diesels in multiple, 10000 10001. Although shunting went on in the adjoining yards, there was just one local freight. No fewer than 108 of these trains were express passenger, of which about two-thirds were to or from Blackpool. I had a current Bradshaw timetable on which I mainly depended for identification of these, but no working timetable or special traffic notice to provide me with details of the 'reliefs' etc."*

Lostock Hall Black 5, 45305, at platform 9 during the course of a B.R. Public relations exhibition of the post steam modernisation programme, on July 24, 1968. The driver, Richard Kay, is on the platform, and fireman, Jock Cummings, is leaning out of the cab. The face peering out from behind the tender is that of Harold Sedgebeer, the last shed master at Lostock Hall. *(Tony Gillett)*

*"On Saturday, August 1, 1959, I first spent 260 minutes (09.25 – 13.45) relishing the amazing traffic on the Fylde lines at Salwick. In that time 138 trains passed, almost all of them expresses to and from Blackpool, with some obviously racing each other on the four-track section to Kirkham & Wesham. I then spent the afternoon (14.15 – 19.15) at Farington, then two hours back at Preston station. At Farington I was in a good position to see what was passing over the bridge carrying the East Lancashire line over the North Union. In 150 minutes, (14.50 - 17.20) no less than 79 movements occurred (10 on the E.L.) 52 of which were express passenger trains, 4 of which being on the E.L. Not a lot had changed in the six years since 1953. There were no more LYR types to be seen; but there were more B.R. Standard locomotives around, with 2 x 2-10-0's working expresses. The L.N.E.R. was represented by five B1's and a K1. There were no 0-6-0's on passenger trains, but some of them were being worked by 2-8-0's, with one being an ex-W. D. Austerity. The unwelcome appearance of Diesel haulage was just beginning, with 5 expresses made up of DMU sets, and one each hauled by type 2 and type 4 locos. Two freights did manage to penetrate Preston that day."*

45336 passes the gantry with the 16.10 Manchester Victoria to Blackpool North/ Fleetwood, on June 8, 1959. *(Ben Brooksbank)*

A brace of 'foreigners' in the form of North Eastern class K3 moguls, 61853 and 61975, haul a Blackpool special on the return leg of the journey in 1964. Note the timber-clad hydraulic accumulator between the bridge and retaining wall. *(Ben Brooksbank)*

*"By 1960, Preston began to be less interesting, as type 4 Diesels were progressively taking over the W.C.M.L. Expresses and more of the Blackpool traffic were being handled by DMU's. A train-watcher did, however, appreciate the early DMU's, because if you managed to secure a seat up front, you had a far better view for number-spotting than was ever possible from an ordinary coach. On Saturday, August 13th, 1960, a year after my previous session, not much had changed. In 4 ½ hours (10.50 – 15.15) I noted 170 workings of which 127 were expresses and just two of freight. I saw only one main line Diesel, and nine DMU's, which were mostly on local trains. Three B1's and three K1's passed with two of them double-heading an express from Leeds/Bradford to Blackpool and back. The London Midland Region was relatively backward in taking up B.R. Standard steam locomotives and , subsequently, I only saw six examples, four of them being 2-10-0's on expresses."*

An unidentifiable Black 5 storms the bank with a train of fish empties for Fleetwood. *(Jack Hodgkinson)*

*"On Saturday, September 8th, 1962, during the Blackpool illuminations, it was even more hectic – if that was possible. In 60 minutes (10.40 – 11.40) there were 28 passenger trains (mainly expresses), and two freight trains. I then went to Kirkham & Wesham, and in 135 minutes (11.55 – 14.10) I saw 44 trains, 34 of which were expresses, with 17 'Illumination Specials.' Finally, back at Preston for another hour (14.20 – 15.20) I saw 13 expresses. As always, Black 5's and other ex-L.M.S. locomotives dominated, with only two B1's; and B.R. Standards comprised merely two Britannia Pacifics, one 4MT 4-6-0 and one 2MT 2-6-2. There were also two Austerities. Moreover, while other parts of the system were being relentlessly Dieselised, I noted (unenthusiastically) a mere five type 4's, only one of which was seen at Kirkham, also a type 2, D5843, from the Eastern Region, and one of the strange type 2, Metrovik Co-Bo's. There were still only nine DMU's on stopping trains."*

*"On Saturday, August 17, 1963, about 175 minutes (12.27 – 15.09) at Preston, followed by 150 minutes (15.17 – 17.47) at Leyland, produced 83 expresses – considerably fewer than in earlier years – the rest being various local trains and no less than eight freights and other workings. It was still fascinating notwithstanding the fact that 25 main line Diesels and 11 DMU's passed through. So the pattern was changing, even if Black 5's (37 of them) dominated the scene. Steam was still abundant in the North-West through 1965, but my observations of Saturday, July 23, 1966 were distinctly depressing. In 282 minutes (10.30 – 15.12) I recorded 115 workings, but 63 of these were Diesels and 26 were DMU's, plus 2 shunters. Nevertheless, I still recorded as many as 26 Black 5's during that stint."*

A Stanier 2-6-4 tank approaches Maudland with a mixed train. *(Jack Hodgkinson)*

Jubilee 45742, Connaught, at Platform 3. *(Arthur Haymes)*

A titled foreigner in the form of Class A1 pacific, 60131, Osprey, heads south on the through lines with a rake of N.E. Stock. *(Arthur Haymes)*

A Black 5, 44759, hurries through the station with a north bound train of fitted vans. *(Arthur Haymes)*

Royal Scot class loco, 46155, entertains the spotters on the 'Glass Bridge' with a southbound train. *(Stan Withers)*

Jubilee, 45714, Revenge, gets under way with a train for the north. *(D. Dyson)*

Within 5 years of the end of steam traction, the surviving railway system in the Preston area had been radically transformed. In 1973, platforms 1 and 2 had been closed to passengers, and disconnected from the main footbridge, with part of the the former waiting rooms and offices having been taken over by the Red Star parcels service, which was sometimes fondly referred to as 'Moscow Parcels' (some years later, the main part of the building was converted to offices for the Civil Engineering Dept.). The platform numbering was subsequently altered, with the main platforms becoming 3 and 4 etc. The East Lancashire side was closed down in the same year, and the main station roof was cut back at the south end. The power signal box, which was built on the site of the engine shed, opened on October 21, 1972, and the old signal boxes in the area were closed down in stages from November, 1972 to February, 1973. Overhead electrification from Crewe to Carlisle was completed in 1974. The men had to learn about the dangers of working beneath the wires and, inevitably, it became a subject for black humour. The following ditty was discovered chalked on the interior of a brake van in the North Union yard, close to the coal-fired stove:

*'If you want to have an electric fire, Lift the stove-pipe two foot higher.'*

## Parcels, mail and goods

A large block of offices at the south end of the main platform was used by the Post Office for sorting and sending letters and parcels. Most of the sorting was carried out at night and then loaded directly into the trains, which was a lot more convenient and quicker than having it carried from the G.P.O office in town to the station. It was calculated that some 2 ½ million letters and 70,000 parcels were sorted and forwarded at the station every week. The railway had its own parcels office, which was located in the 1903 building on Butler Street. In the early 60's, mail bags were conveyed between the main platform to a modern G.P.O. Sorting office on West Cliff Terrace by way of a closed-in bridge, which passed through Christian Road warehouse (part of the top storey at the south end had to be removed to allow for this). The bags were carried on hooks attached to an endless belt.

By 1885, there were three goods sheds in the vicinity of the station, a single storey transship shed and five-storey bonded warehouse on the East Lancs. side at Butler Street, and a two-storey general goods warehouse at Christian Road. The first goods shed on the west side of the station was built by the N.U. on what was then Charles Street. The L.N.W. modified the building in the 1870's and, as space was at a premium, it had to be squeezed in between West Cliff and the Dock branch. With over 200 freight movements a day, there was no room in the vicinity of the station for the making up of all trains, so the bulk of Christian Road traffic was dealt with at Farington, Ribble Sidings (on the south side of the river), and the North Union yard, which had 8 sidings and a loop, just to the south of Christian Road yard, on the site of the original N.U. stables. These sidings were later increased to 13, (10 terminal and 3 straight through). The old N.U. shed was served by two straight-through roads, with a rake of 7 sidings on the west side and 3 on the east side. A series of wagon turntables and a 'triangle' at the rear facilitated the order of wagon disposal and train making. There were 8 jib cranes in the warehouse and 4 in the yard, together with two weighing machines.

The replacement warehouse, which had 3 longitudinal hipped roofs of different lengths, with cut-back and angled walls at the south-east end, was much bigger and the number of internal tracks was doubled to 4, which all terminated within the building. An additional 15 jib cranes were installed, bringing the total to 23. There were 4 ground floor loading bays and 3 external jigger hoists on the west elevation; two loading bays and one jigger on the east elevation, and the same number at the rear. There were also 3 internal jigger hoists. A second, smaller warehouse was built on the site of the turn-table triangle a few yards to the north of the building. It comprised 4 gabled roofs, diminishing in length to the east, and I guess it might have been a transition shed for perishables, such as fruit and vegetables. Beyond this, snugged up in the top corner against the Dock branch wall, was the Anglo-American Oil Company's depot, with storage tanks and workshop etc. Over to the west there was a single track travelling crane with a maximum capacity of 22 tons, and a 5 ton yard crane adjacent to the main warehouse. An extensive stabling accommodation for railway horses followed the north side of the Dock branch curve, between Walton's Parade and the approach at the south end of Christian Road. As with many other goods warehouses, structural and track alterations and modifications were made throughout the L.M.S. and B.R years. The goods agent for both Christian Road and Butler Street in the early 1950's was a Mr. T. Grimes. The chief clerk was a Mr. John Wray, with 40 years service in Preston, and the chief foreman was a Mr. T. J. W. Cousins. There were 73 clerks, 9 supervisors and 220 conciliation grades. In an average month, they would have dealt with 20,940 tons (8,328 wagon loads) of general merchandise; 94,466 tons (9,169 wagons) of coal and coke, and 5,718 tons (654 wagons) of mineral traffic. Just prior to 1950, there were 32 motorised vehicles and 18 horses working at Butler Street and Christian Road depots, and a further 29 horses working internal station duties, such as cartage and transshipping. Freight traffic declined rapidly in the 1960's as a result of competition from the growing number of road haulage contractors, and the devastating effects of the Beeching report. The building was closed, together with those at Butler Street in 1973, with all freight operations being transferred to Blackburn. Demolition followed shortly after, to make way for a larger Post Office sorting and distribution centre.

Driver Jack Cray (left) and no, not young Adolph, but Walter (Rocky) Thompson take 5 for the photographer at Christian Road yard in the late 1950's. Rocky is mimicking Jack by wearing a false moustache. They were the best of mates and a good footplate team. *(Courtesy, Walter Thompson)*

Super D, 49141, prepares for a trip to Heysham on April 17, 1962. *(Tony Gillett)*

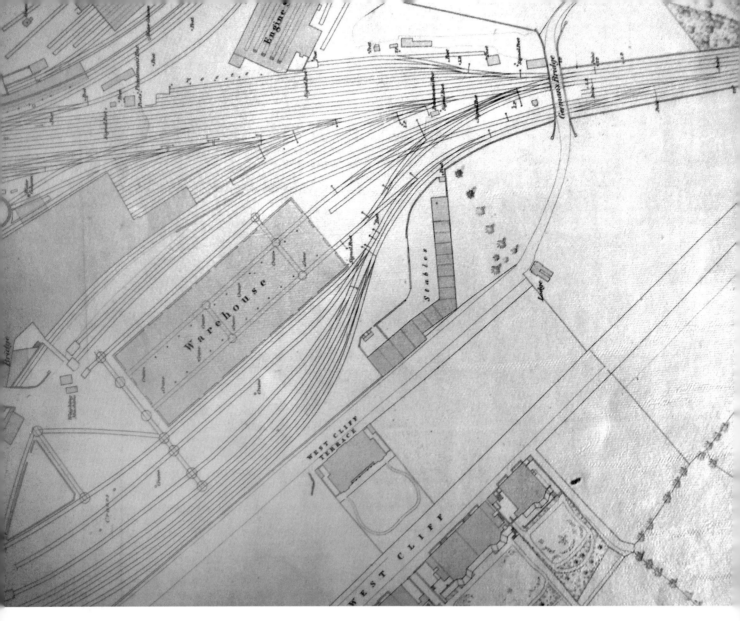

Memo signed by the station master, Mr. J. Hood, with a picture of the fine man himself. (*Author's collection*)

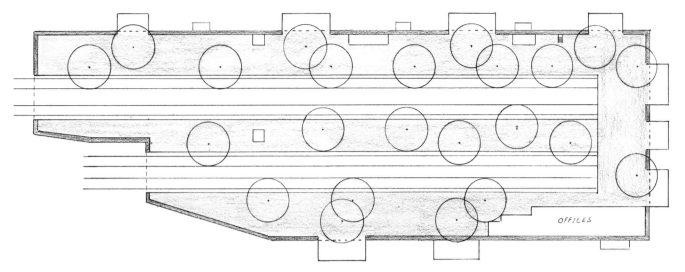

Plan of Christian Road warehouse, showing location of jib cranes and loading bays. *(Author)*

A variety of motive power at the south end, comprising D310, Cravens D.M.U.
and  Black 5, 44776, on April 20, 1961 *(Tony Gillett)*

Winter daydreams. Station pilot, 47413, in the twilight, on December 4, 1960. *(Tony Gillett)*

## Signalling the Station and Main Lines

Preston 2A box (The Bird Cage). *(F. W. Shuttleworth)*

A new signal box was built at Euxton Junction, following the construction of additional tracks in 1880, and was replaced with a larger box following the widening south of the junction in 1894. It was a type 'O' design with an 84 lever frame. The coal sidings box at Euxton was built in 1881 with a Saxby & Farmer frame, which was replaced by a L.N.W. tumbler pattern frame in 1908. Leyland Station box was erected in 1882 and had a 30 lever frame. The next box down the line was Bashall's Siding, which opened in 1880 and served a short branch to Farington Mills. The Saxby & Farmer frame was replaced in 1916 by a L.N.W. design around the same time that a branch line was put in to serve the

Leyland Motor factory. With the opening of the south junction at Farington in 1886, a total of four new boxes were built jointly by the L.N.W. and L.Y. R. companies, with a new junction box being erected in 1910. This was a L.N.W. type 5 with an 84 lever tappet frame, which eventually replaced three of the old boxes. Farington Curve Junction box was built in 1891 for the connecting line to Liverpool via Ormskirk, and later on, in 1908, the East Lancashire curve to Blackburn via Lostock Hall and Bamber Bridge. The latter enabled trains from Lancaster and the north to travel to Blackpool and Fleetwood without stopping at Preston to allow for the locomotives to run round the train and use the turntable. It was also a convenient way of transferring goods from the docks and Christian Road to Butler Street. The box had 30 levers, 27 of which were operational, and was somewhat confined, being narrow and cramped-up against a road bridge, which restricted the signalman's view of the junction. Skew Bridge was the next box down the line. It was constructed following the widening in 1880, and controlled access to the down goods loops, which connected with Ribble Sidings. The Saxby & Farmer box was replaced by a L.N.W. design in 1902, having 36 levers. Ribble Sidings box was erected in 1880 with 65 levers and replaced by an all timber design with 84 levers in 1900, when further widening took place. This box was, in turn, replaced by a L.M.S. design with 50 levers, which was transferred from Southport in 1953.

A post-steam view of Preston No. 4 box on June 5, 1969.
Part of the Diesel stabling point is visible on the west side. *(H. C. Casserley)*

The original Preston No. 1 box was built in 1880, and replaced in 1901 by a large L.N.W. type 'U', with 138 working and 24 spare levers. It had a length of 96 ft 6 ins., with a platform elevation of 18 ft. It was located adjacent to the retaining wall on the up side and controlled the south end of the station. Preston No 1A box was built in 1900, slightly to the north of No. 1, on the down side, and in close proximity to a water tank. It was a small box with a 30 lever frame and controlled traffic to and from the N.U. and Christian Road goods yards. The signalman here also kept the token for single-line working on the Dock branch. Preston No. 2 was constructed in 1882 and located up in the 'Gods' above the island platforms 3 and 4. It had 39 levers and controlled the cross-overs on the down side between platforms 4 and 5. Preston No. 3 was constructed in 1880 and located at the south end of the island platforms 7 and 8. It had 43 levers and controlled the cross-overs on the up line between platforms 6 and 7.

A panoramic view of Maudland during a quiet period, with the No. 5 box on the right and the derelict, roofless engine shed in the left background. The Longridge lines curve away to the right and the beautiful spire of Saint Walburg's dominates the horizon. The picture was taken on August 28, 1964. *(J. A. Coltas)*

Preston No. 2A was another elevated box, located between platform 1 and Christian Road goods warehouse, bestriding the dock branch. It had 69 levers contained within a special frame, and controlled the south end of platforms 1 and 2 and the through lines. It was fondly referred to as the 'Bird Cage,' and the signalmen always had some rotten eggs on hand to hurl at footplatemen who deliberately brought their engines to a halt directly beneath the box with the intention of smoking-out all within. There was a small cabin at Strand Road, with a ground frame, which controlled the crossing and lines leading into the dock area. Preston No. 4 was located north of Fishergate bridge and was the largest box in the Preston area. It became the longest box on the L.N.W. following an extension in 1909, which gave it a total length of 101 ft. It was built in 1902 with a 162 lever frame and a platform elevation of 10 ft., which enabled the signalmen to see what was going on beyond the great bulk of the Fishergate bridge. Another 22 levers were added in the 1909 modifications, bringing the total to 184. This box also controlled a section of the through line to Preston East Lancs. A new frame was installed in 1948 and the total of working levers was increased to 168. The box also contained 15 telephones, 18 block instruments, 8 route-indicators and 6 'Vehicle on Line' indicators. By 1952, the staff comprised 3 signalmen and a lad (train-booker) on early and late turns, and two signalmen and a lad on nights. The men were assisted by 3 illuminated track diagrams which operated in conjunction with a track-circuit system. Access to the box was by way of a centrally located flight of steps on the east side.

Preston No. 5 was another large box, similar in design to No 1, and was located on the up side close to the Longridge branch junction at Maudland. It was opened in 1901 with a 126 lever frame (94 working and 32 spare) and had a platform elevation of 16 ft., accessed by way of an internal staircase. As well as the Longridge branch, it controlled the Fylde junction and access to the engine shed; it also jointly operated the large signal gantry with No. 4. All the distant arms on the gantries were fixed in the on position, as there was a speed limit of 20 mph from the north end of the Ribble bridge to Maudland. The next box on the Lancaster line was Green Bank Sidings, which was built in 1902 prior to the quadrupling of the main line between Preston and Broughton. It had a frame containing 36 working and 24 spare levers. A box was opened at Oxheys in 1902 and controlled sidings into the cattle market. It was removed in 1923 to make way for a bridge carrying the new Blackpool by-pass road, and a new L.N.W. type 5 box with a 50 lever frame was erected close to the new bridge.

Signalman, Jack Tye (right) and his train-booker in Preston No. 4 box. *(Courtesy, Bob Tye)*

Three Preston railwaymen who received an  award for working beyond their retirement in 1940,
up to the end of the second world war. Seated left to right, Ned Pincock, signalman at Euxton Junction;
Jack Tye, signalman at Preston No. 4. Centre, Tommy Ibbert, guard.
The photo was taken at the area manager's office on the station. *(Courtesy, Bob Tye)*

Number 4 box interior. Bob Sowerby, father-in-law of Lostock Hall driver, Ernie Heyes, is in the centre background, wearing a Fair Isle pullover. *(Courtesy, Margaret Heyes)*

47472 is busy making up a train, while the bobby on the elevated No. 3A box gets some fresh air, on May 28, 1960. Would that be someone's initials on the side of the tank, or a derisive exclamation? *(Tony Gillett)*

On the Fylde line, the first box was Maudland Viaduct, which opened in 1889 and had a Railway Signalling Company frame of 42 levers. Maudland Curve box was located between the Lancaster Canal and the bridge carrying Cold Bath Street over the Longridge branch. It was a L.N.W. type 4 design with 15 levers, built in 1882, and controlled the line to Deepdale and the goods yard at Maudland. It was destroyed by fire in 1965. Deepdale Junction was another L.N.W. type 4 box with a 21 lever tumbler frame, which was replaced by a tappet frame in 1926. It controlled the crossing on Skeffington Road and the back-shunt into Deepdale yard.

Preston men were required to work all the boxes as far as and including the one at Garstang & Catterall. Retired railwayman, Bob Tye, recalled the days when his father, Jack, walked the 10 miles to Garstang from his home in Preston on a regular basis, when working the early shift. He would set off from his home at Maudland around 3 o'clock in the morning and walk down the line. Bob's nephew, James Tye, was a lamp man, and it took him half a day to maintain the signal lamps on the large gantry to the north of the station. Each petroleum lamp had to have the wick trimmed or replaced, the reservoir topped-up and the lenses wiped inside and out. An unpleasant and often frustrating job on a cold and windy day. The central station was frequently referred to by 'foreign' enginemen as 'Stop-em-all Junction', owing to the practice of stopping through trains during particularly busy periods.

Number one Crab, 42700, with a train for the Fylde on April 20, 1962. *(Tony Gillett)*

Black 5, 45388, stands at platform 5 (todays platform 3) having backed down onto the 20.50 service to Blackpool South, which was a portion of the 17.05 from London Euston on July 20, 1968. The locomotive had been cleaned at Lostock Hall by enthusiasts prior to the working. *(G.W. Sharpe)*

Black 5, 45448, with a safety valve feathering, leaves Preston with an excusion bound for Blackpool on September 8, 1962. *(Ben Brooksbank)*

Britannia Pacific 70011, Hotspur, awaits the road with the Liverpool/Manchester Express on July 23, 1966. *(Ben Brooksbank)*

Riddles Standard 4, 75046, enters Preston station with a train from Fleetwood and Blackpool North on August 17, 1963. The trains destination was Manchester Victoria. *(Ben Brooksbank)*

A nocturnal scene with Patriot, 45546, Fleetwood, on November 14, 1960. *(Tony Gillett)*

Coronation Pacific, 46257, City of Salford, with an up express on February 20, 1961. This locomotive, together with 46256, was introduced in 1947 and pertained to the Stanier design, with modifications specified by the C.M.E, H.G. Ivatt. *(Tony Gillett)*

Fleetwood Crab, 42765, with an evening parcels
train on November 21, 1960. *(Tony Gillett)*

Ivatt class 2 between station pilot duties on June 6, 1961. *(Tony Gillett)*

Stanier Princess Coronation Pacific, 46227, Duchess of Devonshire,
restarting a through frieght train, July 1961. *(Authors Collection)*

Rebuilt Royal Scot, 46105, Cameron Highlander, with a train from Manchester to Glasgow
on September 8, 1962. *(Ben Brooksbank)*

Members of the Preston schoolboys football team and officials - including the engine driver and guard - pose
in front of a Jubilee locomotive, before travelling to London for a cup final against West Ham in 1936.
A 13 year old Tom Finney is standing on the left side of the buffer beam, wearing shorts. He was a reserve
player on that occasion. *(Lancashire Evening Post)*

An evocative picture of Maudland at night, June 13, 1964. *(Tony Gillett)*

The last officially scheduled standard gauge steam hauled passenger train in the United Kingdom stands at platform 6 in Preston Station on the evening of August 3, 1968. *(Alan Castle)*

# FOOTNOTES.

(1) Preston Guardian, March 13th, 1880.

(2) Preston Chronicle, October 6th, 1860.

(3) **Colonel Yolland. 1810 – 1885.**
William Yolland, Lieutenant-Colonel in the Royal Engineers. He was appointed inspector of railways under the Board of Trade in July 1854 and became chief inspector of railways in 1877, following the retirement of Sir Henry Tyler. In 1880, he was appointed a member of the commission which held an inquiry into the Tay Bridge disaster of December 26th, 1879, and subsequently determined the maximum wind pressure which railway structures should be able to withstand.

(4) **Railway Passenger's Assurance Co.**
The company at that time had a paid up capital and reserve fund of £180,000 and an annual income of £300,000. It was established on December 5th, 1848, as the Universal Railway Casualty Compensation Company. It was re-named some 3 days later, and registered on March 17th, 1849. The company received its first claim following an accident between Preston and Penrith. The claimant was William Good of Dunstable, who was awarded £7 6s. Insurance policies were sold together with tickets by the booking clerks at most main line stations. The company was dissolved on December 23th, 2005. The agent in Preston for 1876 was Arthur J Newbound of 18 Chapel Walk, Preston. Accident statistics for all the nation's railways from 1874 to 1876: 3,928 persons killed and 16,762 injured from all causes. Of that number, 484 killed and 5,760 injured were passengers, and 2,249 killed and 10,305 injured were railway servants.

(5) Corticine: a brown coloured, non-slip linoleum, which was later used on the iron battleships in place of timber decking.

(6) William Sugg & Co. 1837 – 1969. Manufacturers of gas lamps for domestic, public and industrial purposes. The company became the main supplier to the railway companies throughout Britain from the 1800's to the late 1960's. The company was taken over in 1969, and is still producing Victorian style lamps, based on the original designs. Gas lighting was first used in this country by William Murdock, when he was working for Boulton & Watt in 1802. The German inventor, Friedrich Albrecht Winzer, who Anglicized his name to Frederick Albert Winsor, Improved upon the design and introduced public lighting on January 2, 1807 with a colonnade of gas-burning lamps in Pall Mall. Preston became the second place outside London to have its streets illuminated by gas lamps in 1825. The Preston Gaslight Company was founded by Joseph Dunn in 1816. When the L.M.S.R. took over the station in 1923, they replaced the Sugg, Westminster pendant lamps with the 'Littleton' pattern, which had hexagonal opal glass shades.

(7) The station was extended again in 1903, when new platforms and offices were constructed on the East and west sides. Platform 10 was served by a through line, which ran beneath the the booking and parcels offices on Butler Street, and three bay platforms for local trains were built at the south end. For a more detailed account of this side of Preston station, refer to 'The Lancashire & Yorkshire Railway around Preston,' by the same author.

(8) For a more detailed account of the Park Hotel, refer to 'The Lancashire & Yorkshire Railway around Preston,' by the same author.

(9) Preston Guardian, June 27th, 1885. The article mentions the track as being double and laid from the 'General Station'. This would not have been feasible without incurring great cost. It would have been more practicable to run the track from the cattle market. Taking a branch off at Deepdale would have been another possibility.

(10) Dining room staff and women volunteers at Preston station administered refreshments, clothing and cash to soldiers returning from the Crimean war in 1854. See James Byrnes testimonial.

(11) Hewitson, History of Preston.

(12) It appears to have been quite a common practice for senior officers to take up the proprietorship of licensed premises following their retirement from the railway.

(13) Ben. W. L. Brooksbank, renowned railway photographer, was born in Gloucestershire not far from the Birmingham – Bristol L.M.S. line. He began his systematic train-watching records just before the war of 1939, and later moved to London, where he spent most of his adult life. His photographic achievements are just as impressive and meticulous as his record-keeping, and I am grateful to him for allowing me to use one or two in this publication.

# CHAPTER FIVE

# The Engine Shed

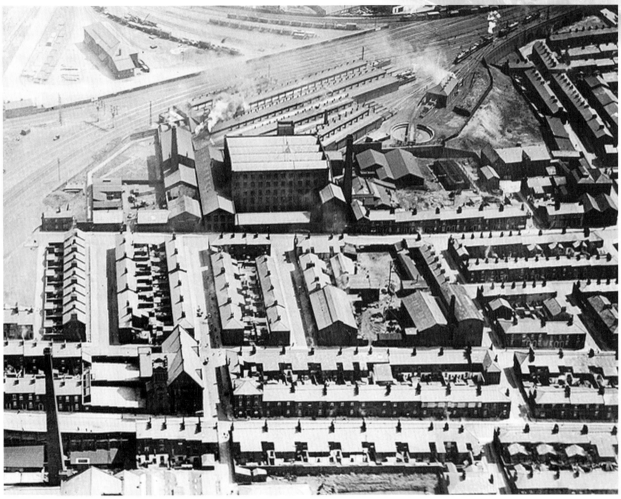

Aerial view of shed taken in 1920. *(British Railways Board)*

The first engine shed at Preston was built by the North Union in 1838, and was located in close proximity to Syke Road bridge. With the arrival of the Lancaster & Preston Junction railway, a shed was constructed somewhere in the vicinity of Dock Street, but the exact location is not known. The only shed for which there is a substantial amount of information, apart from that belonging to the Preston & Wyre Railway at Maudland, is the L.N.W.R. structure of 1872. The estimate, submitted on February 18th, 1871, came to £13,150, and construction work commenced in April 1872. The roofing and smoke-extraction systems were designed by the company's C.M.E., John Ramsbottom , and comprised longitudinal hipped pattern roofs with tall smoke-stacks. Engine Sheds at Wigan and Carnforth were constructed around the same time, in accordance with Webb's transverse gable design.

The shed had 9 roads to begin with and was given the code number 27. A further 6 roads were added in the late 1880's, and along with the turntable and coaling stage, that was about all that could have been crammed into such a confined corner. Preston was designated a sub shed of Springs Branch in 1935, and the code was subsequently changed to 10B. In 1936, the L.M.S. installed a concrete coaling plant and steel-framed ash plant on the west side of the shed, which involved the removal of 6 roads. At the same time, the old L.N.W. roof was demolished and the remaining 9 roads were covered by longitudinal gabled roofs. The shed code changed again for the last time in 1958 to 27K.

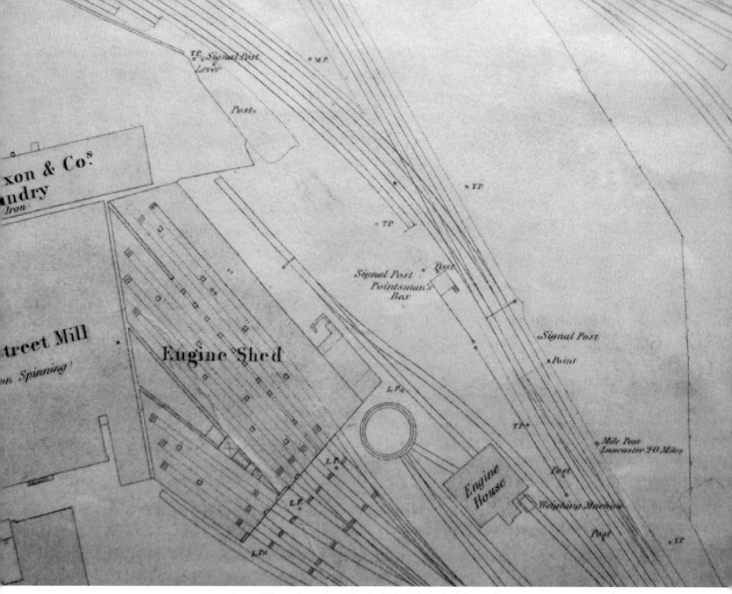

Plan of engine shed, 1862. *(Harris Library)*

Ex – L.N.W. 4-6-0, bearing L.M.S. Number 5781, on shed in the 1930's. *(Geophoto)*

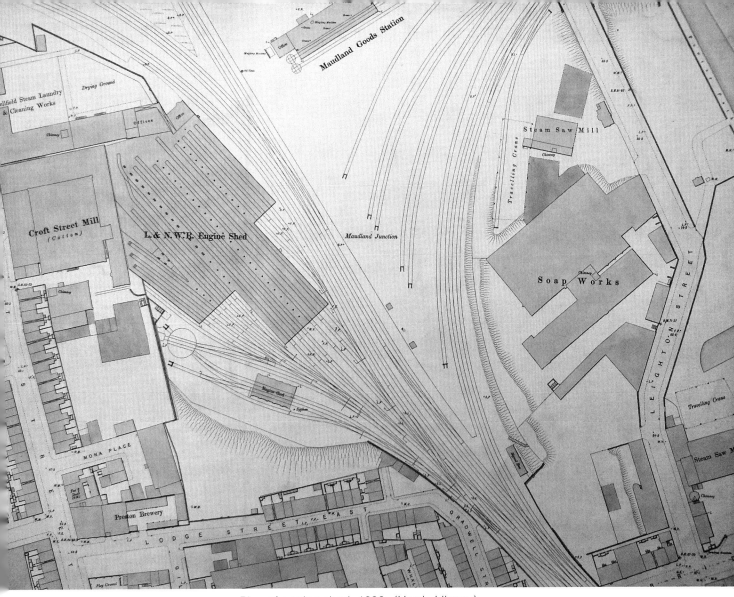

Plan of engine shed, 1892. *(Harris Library)*

The 1923 grouping brought ex-Midland and Lancashire & Yorkshire locomotives to the shed.
Former L & Y Barton Wright 0-6-0, 12063, in the 1930's. *(Geophoto)*

Dreadnought, 10457, on shed circa 1931. *(J.Suter)*

Preston enginemen pose in front of
un-named Patriot, 5544, in LMS days.
Left to right: Dick Riding, Charlie Martindale,
Jack Reeder, Jim Fish, John Hothersall,
Cliff Firth, Unknown fitter, Bob Arkinsall,
George Swift. *(Courtesy, Walter Thompson)*

Perfect number. 45678, De Robeck,
on a visit from Carlisle. *(Tony Gillett)*

Ex- Preston engineman, Bryan Daggers, gives a fascinating account of his time at the shed:

*"I left school at Christmas, 1950 aged 15 years and applied for a job with the railway. I was interviewed and sent to Manchester for a medical, and when I arrived there, I discovered there was no medical office as such, just a couple of steam-heated coaches. I passed the medical with an A1 result, and by January 1st, 1951 I was ready to commence work with British Railways. The engine sheds at Croft Street, where I had spent many happy days watching the locomotives, were just round the corner from where I lived, and as I was on my way to work for the first time, I felt very proud to be working with people who I had got to know personally, such as engine drivers and firemen etc. Most of these men lived locally and I remember them wishing me all the best in my first job. I reported to the time office and was given a metal disc with a number on it, and told to look after it as the disc had to be handed in at the end of the shift, being part of the clocking on/off system."*

Ex - L.N.W. 0-6-0 coal engine, 8525 in L.M.S days. *(Geophoto)*

Class G2, 0-8-0, 'Super D' 9311, in the 1930's. *(Frank Dean)*

*"I wasn't the only new boy to start at the shed that day. There were two others, Frank Hull, who already had two of his brothers working at the shed as firemen, and Bernard Walsh, whose father was a top link driver. Our first job was engine cleaning, which was not subject to any laws pertaining to health and safety; and we were each issued with a bucket of 'Blue Dick' (a mixture of thin oil and paraffin) and a handful of waste-rags. No gloves or skin protection of any kind were given out as a precaution against dermatitis. When cleaning the boiler, we used one rag to apply the mixture and another to wipe it off, which involved having to make bodily contact with the boiler whilst reaching up to clean the crown, which resulted in our clothing becoming wet and filthy. Dinner time soon came round and we were shown how to clean our hands with paraffin and sand. I had the presence of mind to bring along a plug of soap, which had been cut from a large slab, rather like a piece of cheese. We were each issued with a hand cloth, which had to be returned to the stores at the end of the shift and exchanged for a new one."*

Proud Preston Firemen, Dave Williams (left) and Frank Priestley. *(Tony Gillett)*

*"As the months went by, I became familiar with the workings at the shed and soon began to earn more money by labouring, when the yard labourers were off sick or on holiday. One of the jobs which I had to do on a frequent basis was scrubbing the floor in the general office. I started at 5 30 a.m. and by the time I had finished, the floor was white as snow. Today, of course, it would be carpeted. Another job I had was to crawl into the firebox, armed with a 'duck lamp,' hand brush and toffee hammer in order to clean the stays and tube-plate which, once done, would be ready for brick-arch inspection. This was known as the 'Bar lad's' job. I also worked as a sandman, which involved drying out wet sand and ensuring that it was of suitable quality to be poured into the locomotive sand-boxes. The sand was dried out in cone-shaped hoppers with a stove and chimney in the middle. Sometimes I would go for a ride out to the water troughs at Brock with the foreman and two other cleaners on a*

Preston shed from St. Walburg's tower. (Author's collection)

*special train consisting of an engine, three wagons and a guards van. Once there, we quickly unloaded bags of chemicals which were needed to soften the feed water, and because of the acute timing of northbound trains, we could only unload a few bags at a time before taking refuge in the goods loop until it was clear to go back on the main line. All the extra labouring duties were a good boost to my wage, which wasn't bad for a lad just coming up to 16."*

Taking a break in the mess room. Paul Ryan (left) and Alan Pitcher enjoying a brew and a fag on January 13, 1961. *(Tony Gillett)*

44767, doing a turn on May 6, 1961. *(Tony Gillett)*

Close-up of 44767's motion with outside Stephenson's link. *(Tony Gillett)*

*"There were no pay packets in those days, the men received their wages in small circular tins, each bearing a different number on the lid. One of my many tasks was to keep the numbers legible by cleaning the lids with emery paper. At 16, I was ready to be passed out as a fireman, which involved a few days training with the footplate inspector, a gentleman called Bert Fry. This was my first chance of firing at last, and Bert came with me on the Windermere train, giving me plenty of confidence and good advice along the way. We were on the footplate of a Patriot class 4-6-0, No. 45519, Lady Godiva, a great engine! I could see that it was a job where the driver and fireman relied a lot upon each other; team work was a must and there was no time to stand and stare. There was always plenty to do on a footplate, and I followed Bert's instructions to shovel the coal little and often and to watch out for a change in the colour of the smoke at the end of the chimney.*

*As we approached the water troughs at Brock, he told me to listen for the crossing when coming through in the dark, before lowering the scoop, as many a fireman had lowered it too soon, causing damage to the scoop or losing it altogether, resulting in the engine having to be wired off which, in turn, caused delays. I shall never forget that first firing turn, I had a good trip and Bert gave me the O.K., making me a passed cleaner and eligible for local firing turns on a shift system. I started in the 'Monkey Link' on Winter workings, which consisted of eight people clocking on every two hours throughout the day. There was never a shortage of staff, and should a firing turn become available, it was given to the workers who had just booked on, as opposed to the ones who had done so previously. Winter workings always created an abundance of staff, providing us with jobs like looking after the frost fires or 'fire-devils' which were situated next to the water columns at the end of each pit on the shed, and station platforms. I had many a roast potato on this job; they tended to be a bit black, but still all right to eat. Sometimes the foreman would detail about six of us to take coal picks and shovels down to the station and await the arrival of the express train. This was done when the driver of the express had requested coal to be thrown forward in the tender, enabling the fireman to continue his job. This, in turn, enabled the driver to keep to time. We always did our best for the fireman. Two of us would fill the firebox, whist others would work hard in the tender. Within four minutes the train was on its way, with a friendly wave, a loud blast on the steam whistle and the 'thumbs up' sign from the fireman. The next stop for them was Crewe or Carlisle. Some of these trains were twelve to fourteen coaches long, weighing some 450 tons. We would watch them disappear into the darkness of a Winter's night."*

An immaculate, ex-works Black 5, 44762, on a visit from Crewe on June 6, 1961. *(Tony Gillett)*

Class 2P, 40646, takes a drink before working a special on July 1, 1961. *(Tony Gillett)*

*"On returning to the engine shed, we were all as black as the ace of spades, and the foreman was waiting for us with another detail. This time it was 'knocking up,' whereby the the breakdown gang was required to report for work; this was often due to a derailment. We would cycle or walk to the the houses where these men lived, and could not always be certain as to whether we were at the correct address or not. We soon found out, however, if it wasn't, when we got a mouthful of abuse, but we eventually got used to this and the job became more of a good laugh than a trial. In less than an hour the breakdown train would be on its way with all the men on board, and nobody quite certain as to what time they were likely to return. They were dedicated men, despite the moans and groans about their being called out in the middle of the night. Preston shed had its own steam-powered breakdown crane, with the train being made up with two old brake carriages and a tool van.*

*There was a variety of tricks and other mischief that we would get up to. When a train of empty coal wagons left the shed at 4 p.m., the guard would light his stove in the brake van, only to find that we had stuffed waste rags into the stove-pipe. On other occasions, the guard would walk down the length of the train and inform the engine driver how many wagons he had got on. The guard would then give the all clear to move off, and the train would do so, slowly, with the guard leaning on his shunting pole, watching the wagons pass him by (this was common practice, as it saved the guard a long walk back to the end of the train). Unknown to the guard, however, was the fact that we had uncoupled his brake van. It was a treat to see his face when the last wagon appeared, and you should have seen us run! They were happy days."*

Royal Scot, 46145, bearing the long-winded title, The Duke of Wellington's Regiment (West Riding),
. plus coat of arms, reverses out of the yard on May 1, 1961. *(Tony Gillett)*

*"Staff levels remained pretty much constant during the Winter, but as soon as the Summer holidays started, you could find yourself working night and day. Every person in the shed moved up: passed firemen became drivers, regular firemen moved into their places as we, the passed cleaners, became firemen for the Summer period. I was later moved onto the control link, where I had to be available for any job. With the Summer approaching, I was moved on from the Monkey Link to the Barrow and Windermere link. On this job, I found myself firing for non-other than Charles Horam, the father of Wandering Walter. He lived two streets away from me, and his usual greeting was 'All right, Fettler'. Charley was a great guy; he never bothered or questioned me, we just had that understanding and teamwork. I remember Charley shouting at the top of his voice before the train left Windermere, 'All aboard for the Skylark!' This was usually followed up with his favourite song, 'Quai sera sera, what will be will be.' Good old Charley. Also, on behalf of Walter's fans, I would like to wish him all the best on his retirement. This I cannot see, as he still cracks jokes on the radio.*

*Later on in the Summer, I was moved further up to the Top Link, which was the London – Glasgow run, and involved a more serious attitude to work. I would go early to the sheds when working the 10 40 p.m. London train, and usually fired for Sammy Rolls and Frank Edgar. First of all I would look at the shed engine board to see which engine we had been assigned to that night. It was invariably a Royal Scot class. I would spread the fire and fill the firebox to the brim, then go round and oil the motions, big ends etc. underneath, and fill the sand boxes, all of which amounted to a combination of a driver and fireman's duties. This was an instance of how teamwork made the job easier all round. After that, I would move the engine round to the coaling plant and fill the tender to the top, taking care to stake the coal, which saved me from having to dig in the tender at Rugby. After completing these details I would put the engine back into the shed, rush home, have a good wash, put on a clean shirt and go back to work ready for the off. We travelled light engine to Preston where we hooked on to the train , and set off into the darkness. I had to watch how the engine behaved, keeping an eye on the water level and steam pressure. You could always tell how things were going to be after the first ten minutes; the firebox would be all aglow and we would travel at speeds reaching 70 to 80 miles per hour."*

Stanier Pacific, 46240, City of Coventry, cleaned, oiled and ready for the road on May 27, 1961. *(Tony Gillett)*

*"New year's Eve was a good time to be at the shed. We would tie a piece of string to all the whistle levers then, as midnight approached, the levers would be tied down full blast. This terrific noise would be heard all over the town, along with ships' sirens at the docks and church bells. Preston town always welcomed in the new year with good spirit. Going back to running, it always reminds me of Tom Finney, the perfect player. Preston sheds and local shunts were definitely running on Saturdays, and we all rushed to go to the football match to watch our Tom. We would clean the fire whilst waiting at signals, and hurry getting water; anything to get away early, even shouting at the signalman, 'On the shed, Bobbie'. When there was a match on, we would plead with the shed foreman to sign our works ticket, giving us the O.K. to go. In order to reach the football ground quickly, we would cross the main line to Maudland Bank sidings, then walk through the tunnel to Deepdale. The crowds there often numbered 30,000 to 35,000. With black, shiny caps, oily overalls, grubby faces and haversacks containing tea and butties left over from the early morning, we would stand at the town end watching Tom and shouting, ' Give it to Tommy.' There was never any trouble at football matches in those days; you went to a football ground to watch the match. Sometimes the terraces were so packed that I couldn't get my hands into my pockets to eat a sandwich; in fact I got carried away with the game to such an extent, that hunger never even entered my mind. Thanks Tom."*

The fireman poses for his photo by the shed's un-named patriot, 45542,
on March 2, 1961. *(Tony Gillett)*

Handsome engines, these!
Jubilee, 45723, Fearless, south of the yard on March 2, 1961. *(Tony Gillett)*

44766 reverses out of the yard with cylinder cocks full open, on January 26, 1961. *(Tony Gillett)*

The Royal Scot herself, 46100, looking good in the lamp light on October 10, 1961. *(Tony Gillett)*

"1952 was a guild year which brought many special trains into Preston. I can remember working in the loco yard one day, during that time, making sure engines were being marshalled in the correct order for going out. I phoned the shed foreman telling him the yard was full, and he got permission to use the carriage sidings for the overspill near the station, sending along a steam-raiser to keep an eye on them. It was a train spotter's paradise. There were engines from all parts of the country that had never been seen in our neck of the woods before. I didn't see much of the Guild that year, as I was on the afternoon shift, working 4 p.m. to midnight. At 17 years of age, I was eligible for the main line, counting my firing turns at 287, which was the number required to start on first year firing pay, and a big leap from that of the cleaners.

In certain places along the route, the driver would keep his head out in the dark, on the lookout for signals, and not wanting to catch the glare from the fire. It was a thirsty job on the footplate. I always took a can or bottle of tea with me and I knew every water tap between London and Glasgow. When arriving at stations I would jump off and fill my can with cold water. Once all the passengers had disembarked at Euston, we had to back-shunt the train into the sidings and then proceed light engine to Camden shed. We would then book off and go to the railwaymen's hostel, or 'Barracks' as they were better known. I remember looking at my coal-blackened face in the wash room mirror, and hearing two guards having a conversation – I couldn't help noticing their clean, white shirts and cuff links. One of the guards mentioned that he had just worked the 10. 40 from Preston, and I had to bite my tongue. It was the face in the mirror who had worked the train, and didn't I know it – my shirt was wet through with sweat! Still, as they say, it's all in a day's work."

A smart, clean Jubilee, 45648, Wemyss, on March 7, 1962. *(Tony Gillett)*

"One of the worst times for me during my 'double-trip' days was trying to sleep. The barracks at Camden Town were situated adjacent to the shunting yard and it was bang bang bang all day long, which was no joke if you were trying to sleep. The one at Glasgow was a bit better. I remember washing my socks and hanging them out of the bedroom window, only to be questioned by the lady in charge, asking who had room 18. I replied in the affirmative and you should have seen her face as she said, "Don't you think that Glasgow's scruffy enough without you putting your socks out!" Say no more.

The longest trips I ever made were from to Preston via Northampton, during the Summer at weekends. We sometimes had a powerful Duchess class loco on that route. How pleased and proud I felt when running in to Preston station. I would wash my hands and swill the footplate down ready for our relief, and after handing the engine over to them, the driver and I would make our way back to the engine shed on foot, crossing the lines and watching the engine drawing away with her driving wheels slipping and palls of black smoke belching out of the chimney, then soon picking her wheels up and away.

A sign of things to come, in the form of Type 4, No. D7, on January 16, 1961. *(Tony Gillett)*

*Getting away from the graft and loss of sleep, one of the jobs we had at Preston was hauling a train called the 'Pilling Pig.' It was a good day job and the train was made up of coal wagons and a cattle truck. A chap called Mickey Doland was my driver at the time, and he was always good for a laugh. He was only about 5 ft. tall, and to operate the regulator he would get his shoulder under it ; sometimes he would stand on a large cob of coal to give him more height. We would set off from Preston having to move very fast on the main line north, until we arrived at Garstang, and once clear of the main line we entered a different world on our way to Pilling. We passed through some beautiful countryside, stopping at every crossing and waiting for the guard, who was a namesake of mine, Tom Dagger, to walk the full length of the train, so unconcerned that he would stop to stroke a horse or a passing cat. He would then have a chat with the persons who lived at the crossing-keepers' houses, who had once operated the crossings many years ago. I would drop them a cob off, knowing that on the way back we would be given flowers or eggs, or even home-made bread and cakes. They were great people, very friendly and homely. On arriving at Pilling, we were greeted by a dapper of a chap called Arthur Aughton, who was always dressed in a smart uniform, with waistcoat, peaked cap and shiny shoes. This versatile man played the role of station master, porter, chief clerk etc. Once we had shunted our train, we would sit on the grass bank and have a can of tea and some sandwiches. Arthur would join us and tell us different tales. He was a very educated man, well known for writing articles in the Lancashire Evening Post. Incidentally, he lived to a good old age and was remembered by the Evening Post when he died. Always remembered."*

A close-up of 45706's starboard-side brass nameplate, with winged mercury streaking beneath. June, 1961. *(Tony Gillett)*

The coal-hopper, ash plant, disposal pits and turntable were all located in the confines of the north-west corner. Add two or three engines and a rake of coal trucks and you had a fairly crowded environment. 42715, 44907 and 46168, 'The Girl Guide', along with two other engines are receiving attention from the firemen and yard staff on July 1, 1961. *(Tony Gillett)*

"One of the most frightening experiences I ever had, was when I was coming back from Crewe with a fully fitted goods train and approaching Weaver Junction. The semaphore signal could be seen on the fireman's side first. I was firing for Bert Holt at the time and he looked across at me waiting for the all-clear sign, but I could only see red, and shouted, "All on, Bert!" He dashed across the footplate to confirm, then shut off the regulator and applied the brakes, while I applied the handbrake. Sparks were flying and the brakes screeching, but we managed to stop just short of the signal, only to find that it was half-cocked, in other words between off and on! I apologised to Bert, but he looked at me and said, "No need, Bryan, what we did was right, and if we had just taken it for granted and carried on across the junction with a train coming, then we would have done wrong. Think about it, it's better to be safe than sorry," I set off on foot to inform the signalman about his faulty signal. Bert made out a full report about the incident and the next day, the shed boss, Mr. Cunningham, called me in to thank me for being observant and giving me further details of what would have happened if I had failed to do so.

I received my call up papers for National Service when I was 18, and applied to join the Royal Engineers Railway Section at Longmore, but I was very disappointed when I received a reply informing me to report to Ramilies Barracks at Aldershot, on February 4, 1954. Army catering Corps! I could have cried, but a friend of mine (another fireman who, sadly, has since died, Ken Hornby), said, "Don't worry, Bryan," showing me his papers, "I'm coming with you on the same posting." They must have been short of cooks. Aldershot, here we come! During my National Service, I lost all sense of home life and missed seeing North End in the 1954 cup final, and forgot all about the railway. My lifestyle changed rapidly; square bashing and catering training took care of that. I must admit that I was not keen to learn cooking, but I finished up attached to 27 Field Eng. Reg. Royal Engineers in Germany. I helped to cook for General Sir Richard Gayle, who was C/C B.A.O.R. (British Army of the Rhein).Not bad for a railway lad!"

Jubilee 45629, Straits Settlement, on the table. May 27, 1961. *(Tony Gillett)*

The nameplate says it all. A distinguished visitor to the shed on June 17. 1961. *(Tony Gillett)*

"I was de- mobbed in 1956, and soon back on the footplate, picking up where I left off. I remember seeing the Deltic Diesels undergoing their trials on the main line, also Diesels working on the Dock Branch line, that brought up coal, wood, pulp and pit props. It was a steep incline, but they managed it all right and eventually replaced the Super D steam locomotives. The fastest train I ever worked was a very heavy newspaper express from Preston to Carlisle, which travelled 90 miles in 90 minutes. We worked out of Preston double-headed, remembering to share the water when picking up on the troughs. We were relieved at Carlisle. Sometimes we would travel home as passengers on the Glasgow train, but instead of sitting in the coach and taking it easy, I would ask permission to travel on the footplate and help the fireman to put a good fire on. You could never learn enough all the time from being a cleaner to driver."

Not a pleasant task on a cold day! Washing out the boiler on January 9, 1961. *(Tony Gillett)*

Final stages in the life of a Super D, with details of her mechanical history chalked on the boiler. August 9, 1961. *(Tony Gillett)*

"*I enjoyed going to improvement classes; they would be held at least once a fortnight and we would go along in our own time after tea; the lecture would be given by one of the drivers, who would discuss the 'Black Book'. The rule book was a very important guide to all railwaymen and it had to be kept up to date with all the amendments. Another activity I took part in when not working, was football. I played for the shed in the Preston Thursday League. We played on Thursdays because it was half day closing. The teams which took part included Friargate shops, Police, Post Office, Preston Dairies and two army teams from the near-by garrison at Fulwood. Just think, we were up at 4 a.m. then off to Crewe and back, and then had a game of football. Still, we enjoyed it. As you can tell, my story of the railway all revolved around working together, through all conditions, whether good or bad. I'm afraid a man called Dr. Beeching ended all that when he chopped the railway and its staff, and those times were never to come back again. Progress can do that, but it can never remove memories.. 1960 was my last year on the railway; I had decided to find another job and start afresh. The old steam railway has never left me, and my visits to the museum at York bring it all back.*"

"*Once again, to all my ex-railway friends and enthusiasts,* **'ON THE SHED BOBBIE'**      **Happy days.**"

A line of Super D's and Stanier tanks in store awaiting thier fate. 1963/4. *(G. Harrop)*

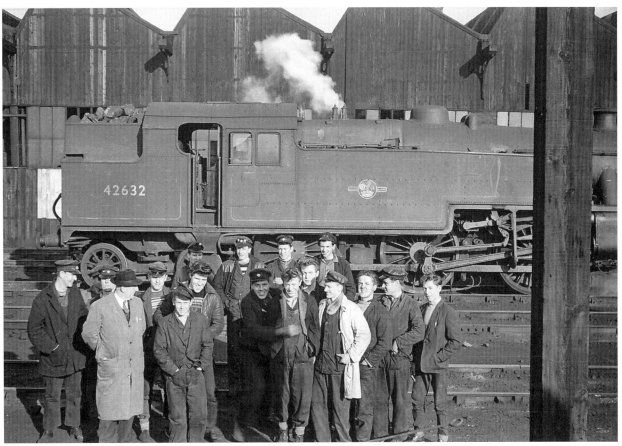

Stanier Class 4 tank, 42632, provides the backdrop for a group photo of Preston lads at Wigan L&Y
Firing School, on February 6, 1961. Tony Gillett only just managed to regain his position at centre-front,
after setting up the camera, with delayed-action, on an adjacent engine.
The result was better than he expected. *(Tony Gillett)*

What can be described as the work of the keen and attentive young fireman, Tony Gillett, following
a Firing School course at Wigan North Western on February 1, 1961. *(The artist himself)*

Driver, Fred Jackson recalls his days at Preston, after having been transferred there from Hellifield:

*"Seniority was the fact that governed all promotion on the footplate and all higher grade work. Passed cleaner to fireman and passed fireman to driver, with the senior man placed first in all daily work. This was a fair system, as route knowledge was also a factor. I soon found that work on the West Coast required a greater degree of skill, and that Preston was a different world! The control link was just the place for me, as there were 12 sets of men of which 4 were top of list, meaning that they were covering for sickness and holidays etc., and the remaining sets were working as required on the control link, which comprised for the most part freight operations. My first trip to London was quite an experience. I booked on with Frank Fletcher, who was then a junior passed fireman. The engine was a Jubilee, 5582 'United Provinces', newly transferred from the Scottish Division; she was very rough and generally in poor condition. We went light engine to Blackpool and backed up to a train of 16 coaches (480 tons) for a R.A.F. special from Lytham to Southampton*

*This was quite a task for both the engine and myself, as I was a stranger to the route and had to be told all the way of what was ahead, such as gradients and troughs. We seemed to be going on forever, about 4 ½ to 5 hours non stop, before being relieved at Willesden; my longest journey prior to this one being of 1 ½ hours duration.*

*Most of the pilot work on express trains was carried out by Midland or L.M.S. class 2P, 4-4-0 locomotives. The Midland types were generally better steamers, but they had no doors between the engine and tender, which made things a bit precarious when going at speed. Train weights were calculated on empty weight, for example, standard bogie coach, parcel/mail van (converted coach), 30 tons; dining car, 50 tons; first class sleeper, 50 tons, third class sleeper, 45 tons; milk tanks, 35 tons.*

*I was soon in the Barrow passenger link with a variety of jobs, mainly express work with the London trains. In those days, many trains were split up or joined up at Preston to work Crewe, Blackpool, Windermere, Carlisle, Manchester etc. This was the prelude to the next link, London to Glasgow, and I soon found myself in it. At Preston shed we had 5XP Jubilee engines, which had been re-classified to 6P, but we always referred to them as 5X's. Apart from the above mentioned 5582, we had 5633, Aden; Patriot, 5519, Lady Godiva, and 5538, Giggleswick, which I deemed to be the best of the bunch. Of the Black 5's, No. 5332 was the best. We also had Super D's for dock work and coal to Fleetwood. Most of our work was diagrammed for Crewe – Carlisle which involved the Camden Royal Scot class locomotives.*

*For the next few years I was working in the London link, firing for Fred Spencer (ex-Royal Engineers), Bob Dickinson, Jack Moss, Harry Preston, Jack Ireton, Joe McMeekin. This was hard work, and at the end of a shift I was 8 ½ stone, wet through, but I loved it. You certainly didn't get fat in this link, and some of the lads exchanged links with me, as they didn't all like this kind of work. Those not familiar with footplate work would find it difficult to imagine the bed and work shift patterns. For example, a typical start to the week would be out of bed at 1.0 a.m. Sunday, then 2.8 a.m. for 2.35 Glasgow; (double trip), arrive Glasgow 4.45 a.m.; book off and back in bed, 9.30 to 10.0 a.m.; up at 5.0 to 6.0 p.m. Meal and relax, then book on at 9.30 p.m. Prepare engine etc. and top up tender with coal, then off Polmadie at 11.0 p.m.; back up to 11.30 Liverpool. Back to Preston at 4.45 a.m. then book off at 5.10 a.m. Home and into bed again at 7.0 a.m. Up in the afternoon, then book on at 11.41 p.m. mad hour commences: 12.9 newspapers to Carlisle, then home; return with Aberdeen to London fish / parcels train. Home at 7.30 a.m. Off till 9.24 Wednesday night, for 10.39 Euston, booking off 6.0 at Camden. Up at 3.0 p.m. and book on at 4.0 p.m. for the 5.35 p.m. Emerald Isle. Thursday, Preston at 11.0 p.m. on the shed, then home and bed again. Book on again on Saturday at 2.8 a.m. for double trip to Glasgow at 2.35 a.m., then return with 11.30 p.m. for Liverpool. Home around 5.30 a.m. and bed. This was just one week's work in the London link. In Winter we never saw daylight except on an afternoon job to Windermere, returning with K-Shoes consignment from Kendal, arriving in Preston at 9.0 p.m. (during the Summer months, this would have been the 12.45 Windermere – Crewe, better known as the Lakes Express). How our bodies withstood the irregular sleep and eating patterns amazes me; when you arrived home at these times, bed was the only option. There was always a set of men going north and another coming south, and we usually passed each other in the vicinity of Oxenholme. I was rarely at home for Christmas, it was just another working day. When my first son was born, he was home from hospital in the afternoon, while I was en-route to Glasgow on the 2. 35 double trip.*

*At 25 years of age, I was through the London link and into the Southport passenger link, which was the one in which we took our driving examinations. I had 11 years seniority, and all the time I was learning the signalling and roads etc. rules and regulations: we were really a disciplined work force, living with the rule book and learning all the time. In the evenings, after my wife had put the children to bed, she would ask me questions from the rule book. Rule 55, very important – 'Detention of trains on running lines'....26 pages of various paragraphs and amendments and you needed to know this rule word for word. The examination began with an oral test in the shed master's office, where Arthur King asked questions on the rule book and other subjects. With this part successfully accomplished, we had a break, then there came the driving test with passenger and goods trains, and finally, Arthur took me round the engine, asking questions of a mechanical nature, and asking me if the engine required any running repairs, which it didn't, and so I became a passed fireman. You were only allowed 3 attempts, and that was that; there was no future on the footplate for failed drivers. On most occasions, a fireman would leave before this happened, but most candidates passed first time."*

## Staff list of footplate grades for Preston M.P.D.

*Not all members of staff are included here, as it pertains to Welfare Club members only.*

| Name | Grade | D.O.B | Seniority Date | Remarks |
|---|---|---|---|---|
| F. Ainscough | Driver | 12/02/05 | 20/03/19 | |
| T. Anderton | Passed Fireman | 06/09/38 | 04/01/54 | |
| G. Ashwin | Driver | 11/09/07 | 31/03/25 | |
| E. Aspin | Driver | 12/06/18 | 08/03/37 | |
| H. Baldwin | Driver | 11/05/04 | 05/06/18 | Shunt only. |
| W. Baldwin | Senior Shed man. W.S.P. Attd. | 24/09/23 | 28/05/51 | Resettlement. |
| A. Barton | Driver | 26/07/25 | 30/03/42 | |
| G. Beardwood | Driver | 24/06/04 | 21/10/18 | |
| J. Bell | Driver | 16/08/28 | 13/08/45 | |
| W. Bell | Driver | 16/09/25 | 10/03/47 | |
| D. Belshaw | Passed Fireman | 10/12/40 | 02/01/56 | |
| T. Belshaw | Passed Fireman | 19/08/36 | 20/08/51 | |
| S. Bennett | Driver | 26/12/18 | 26/01/37 | |
| S. G. Bennett | Passed Fireman | 22/04/40 | 12/04/55 | |
| R. Billington | Driver. | 16/03/30 | 28/01/46 | |
| R. Bonney | Driver | 02/02/05 | 20/03/19 | |
| K. Booth | Foreman's Asst. Class 1 | 27/05/46 | 31/12/56 | |
| J. Boyle | Passed Fireman | 09/04/40 | 12/04/55 | |
| C. Brayshaw | Driver | 30/10/22 | 26/08/40 | |
| W. Buckley | Driver | 10/02/22 | 30/12/40 | |
| C. Bull | Driver | 04/09/18 | 28/12/36 | |
| A. Callaghan | Fireman | 28/02/48 | 26/08/63 | |
| R. S. Calvert | Passed Fireman | 22/07/32 | 28/03/49 | |
| R. T. Calvert | Passed Fireman | 10/06/42 | 12/08/57 | |
| F. Chadwick | Driver | 03/08/04 | 29/01/19 | |
| B. Chamberlain | Fireman | 18/04/43 | 23/01/61 | |
| A. Chesters | Driver | 07/02/28 | 01/03/44 | |
| L. Clitheroe | Driver | 13/10/23 | 17/06/40 | |
| T. Collier | Driver | 05/09/24 | 25/10/40 | |
| D. Cookson | Fireman | 07/05/48 | 22/07/63 | |
| J. Coop | Driver | 09/04/23 | 17/12/40 | |
| J. Cox | Driver | 27/03/17 | 25/01/37 | |
| J. Cray | Driver | 07/04/20 | 02/09/35 | |
| T. Cuthbertson | Passed Fireman | 04/09/34 | 05/09/50 | |
| J. Dean | Driver | 24/09/25 | 15/06/42 | |
| H. Dobson | Shed man | 10/03/05 | 15/11/65 | Ex-workshop grades 15. 11. 65 |
| P. Dolan | Passed Fireman | 27/04/39 | 27/04/54 | |
| V. Drew | Foreman's Asst. Class 1 | 09/02/13 | 27/09/50 | |
| A. Duxbury | Driver | 05/01/23 | 17/07/39 | Shunt only |
| F. Edgar | Driver | 28/07/07 | 16/08/23 | |
| B. Fare | Fireman | 19/05/42 | 27/04/59 | |
| D. Fewery | Passed Fireman | 25/01/32 | 09/02/48 | |
| C. Firth | Driver | 03/02/21 | 23/12/35 | |

| Name | Grade | D.O.B | Seniority Date | Remarks |
|---|---|---|---|---|
| J. Fleming | Passed Fireman | 15/12/47 | 06/09/54 | |
| F. Fletcher | Driver | 21/02/25 | 20/01/41 | |
| J. Gittings | Driver | 18/01/11 | 22/03/26 | |
| A. Goodwin | Driver | 13/05/23 | 12/05/41 | |
| T. Gorman | Passed Fireman | 27/05/41 | 09/07/56 | |
| R. Gorton | Driver | 31/10/23 | 18/12/40 | |
| A. Green | Driver | 02/04/25 | 26/08/42 | |
| R. Green | Driver | 21/12/23 | 25/11/40 | |
| J. Grundy | Driver | 16/01/18 | 08/03/37 | |
| J. Hall | Driver | 10/10/19 | 26/07/37 | |
| G. Harris | Driver | 30/12/15 | 11/10/20 | |
| G. Hetherington | Passed Fireman | 14/04/33 | 02/08/49 | |
| F. Higham | Senior Shed man (W.S.P. Attd.) | 24/09/23 | 28/05/51 | |
| K. Hilton | Passed Fireman | 21/05/39 | 11/06/56 | |
| R. Hobson | Passed Fireman | 07/12/41 | 13/05/57 | |
| J. Hoggarth | Fireman | 30/07/45 | 30/08/60 | |
| S. Hogg | Driver | 26/05/27 | 06/10/42 | |
| W. Holman | Fireman | 01/05/45 | 18/07/60 | |
| K. Hope | Passed Fireman | 03/10/33 | 04/01/54 | |
| K. Hornby | Passed Fireman | 15/11/35 | 31/07/51 | |
| C. Houghton | Fireman | 22/01/48 | 17/08/64 | |
| M. Howarth | Fireman | 24/04/47 | 07/05/62 | |
| A. Hull | Passed Fireman | 25/04/42 | 29/04/57 | |
| D. Huyton | Driver | 08/06/26 | 13/09/43 | |
| R. Jackson | Fireman | 12/05/43 | 17/10/60 | |
| W. Jackson | Passed Fireman | 07/06/26 | 21/03/49 | |
| P. Jameson | Driver | 04/05/30 | 11/06/46 | |
| J. Johnson | Passed Fireman | 21/09/26 | 07/07/48 | |
| L. Just | Driver | 13/12/18 | 25/01/37 | |
| G. Keane | Passed Fireman | 14/11/34 | 22/10/51 | |
| W. Kendall | Passed Fireman | 03/11/36 | 31/12/51 | |
| H. Knott | Fireman | 09/08/46 | 12/11/62 | |
| T. Lee | Driver | 01/12/04 | 15/09/21 | |
| D. Leech | Driver | 19/07/27 | 24/05/43 | |
| G. Lilley | Driver | 06/06/24 | 27/05/46 | |
| A. Malone | Passed Fireman | 30/08/23 | 06/10/47 | |
| K. Mason | Passed Fireman | 12/09/23 | 29/09/47 | |
| S. Maxwell | Driver | 21/03/22 | 04/09/47 | |
| B. Mawson | Driver | 24/01/28 | 09/11/43 | |
| H. McCann | Driver | 16/11/22 | 23/09/40 | |
| O. McCarten | Driver | 20/01/23 | 03/06/40 | |
| K. McIver | Driver | 06/03/30 | 12/08/46 | |
| K. McCrink | Passed Fireman | 20/07/41 | 10/09/56 | |
| J. McDonnell | Driver | 30/04/18 | 02/12/35 | |
| P. McShane | Shed man | 15/08/49 | 25/10/67 | |
| T. Mercer | Shed man | 19/07/01 | 28/01/19 | Over 65 |
| T. Miller | Driver | 22/07/27 | 28/09/42 | |
| K. Mitchell | Fireman | 21/04/42 | 31/08/60 | |
| S. Morley | Passed Fireman | 06/01/39 | 02/05/56 | |
| J. Morris | Passed Fireman | 04/02/37 | 21/04/52 | |
| H. Mounsey | Driver | 02/10/22 | 15/01/40 | |

| Name | Grade | D.O.B | Seniority Date | Remarks |
|---|---|---|---|---|
| J. Neil | Passed Fireman | 12/03/33 | 23/08/49 | |
| B. Nicholson | Driver | 03/01/29 | 12/11/45 | |
| J. Oldham | Driver | 24/04/17 | 27/10/36 | |
| R. Orr | Driver | 09/06/23 | 07/04/47 | |
| R. Owen | Fireman | 20/11/43 | 30/01/61 | |
| L. Parkin | Driver | 12/05/25 | 17/05/43 | |
| W. Prenderguest | Driver | 26/02/19 | 12/03/34 | |
| S. Phillipson | Driver | 06/12/22 | 24/06/40 | |
| A. Porter | Passed Fireman | 26/05/41 | 23/07/56 | |
| J. Raby | Driver | 26/09/23 | 16/04/41 | |
| L. Rampling | Driver | 09/10/29 | 16/12/43 | |
| W. Rawcliffe | Driver | 04/09/19 | 03/06/35 | |
| A. Reddington | Passed Fireman | 14/04/27 | 13/03/50 | |
| F. Roberts | Driver | 12/05/27 | 10/01/44 | |
| T. Robinson | Shed man | 14/12/18 | 29/12/66 | Ex-workshop grades, 15. 11. 65 |
| W. Robinson | Driver | 22/02/18 | 05/08/35 | |
| I. Ross | Fireman | 19/09/45 | 22/10/62 | |
| T. Rudd | Driver | 01/10/31 | 18/08/47 | |
| P. Ryan | Fireman | 24/03/44 | 10/10/60 | |
| F. Salisbury | Driver | 26/05/18 | 02/12/35 | |
| J. Salthouse | Driver | 04/09/26 | 23/08/43 | |
| B. Sanders | Driver | 07/01/23 | 17/07/39 | |
| J. Slater | Passed Fireman | 04. 02, 36 | 08/08/56 | |
| B. Southworth | Passed Fireman | 04/07/35 | 26/11/51 | |
| J. Tattersall | Passed Fireman | 26/06/42 | 29/07/57 | |
| J. Thompson | Passed Fireman | 30/03/39 | 20/04/54 | |
| W. Thompson | Driver | 05/09/18 | 18/11/35 | |
| B. Townsend | Passed Fireman | 10/05/41 | 09/07/56 | |
| J. Walker | Passed Fireman | 12/12/28 | 30/05/49 | |
| A. Watkinson | Driver | 03/02/28 | 31/05/45 | |
| R. White | Passed Fireman | 26/03/40 | 25/07/55 | |
| A. Whittingham | Driver | 12/05/27 | 07/09/42 | |
| E. Williams | Driver | 06/03/30 | 12/08/46 | |
| G. Williams | Driver | 23/04/28 | 06/12/43 | |
| T. Williams | Driver | 23/03/31 | 01/09/47 | |
| W. Wilson | Passed Fireman | 09/04/47 | 23/02/53 | |
| J. Winder | Driver | 30/01/30 | 16/06/47 | |
| A. Wood | Driver | 18/11/29 | 02/04/45 | |

### Staff list of footplate grades for Lostock Hall M.P.D. (Welfare Club members only)

*This list, together with the Shed conciliation grades, has been included, as there was a transfer of staff from Preston to Lostock Hall in 1961, and a reciprocal transfer in 1968.*

| Name | Grade | D.O.B | Seniority Date | Remarks |
|---|---|---|---|---|
| Ainsworth J.A. | Driver | 18/07/27 | 16/05/49 | |
| Allison E. | Driver | 28/03/29 | 03/01/44 | |
| Alty S.R. | Driver | 06/08/27 | 30/11/42 | |
| Anderson W.E. | Driver | 10/09/28 | 06/05/46 | |
| Ashcroft J.E. | Fireman | 31/05/48 | 17/05/65 | |
| Ashton E. | Fireman | 12/03/47 | 07/05/62 | |

| Name | Grade | D.O.B | Seniority Date | Remarks |
|---|---|---|---|---|
| Aspin J. | Driver | 18/05/26 | 30/06/42 | |
| Aston W. | Passed Cleaner | 24/12/48 | 16/01/67 | |
| Bamber W. | Driver | 11/06/29 | 24/04/47 | |
| Bolton H. | Driver | 20/03/31 | 02/06/47 | |
| Brown H. | Driver | 11/01/29 | 03/05/48 | |
| Bowden M. | Driver | 14/08/33 | 20/10/48 | |
| Burke J.H. | Driver | 17/03/29 | 21/06/49 | |
| Burnett J.J. | Driver | 17/10/33 | 19/11/51 | |
| Barron F. | Driver | 17/02/28 | 29/09/52 | |
| Brady J. | Driver | 19/10/31 | 26/01/53 | |
| Blakeley H. | Fireman | 06/12/45 | 23/05/61 | |
| Booth J. | Fireman | 04/03/47 | 07/05/62 | |
| Baxter E.T. | Passed Cleaner | 15/06/48 | 06/03/67 | |
| Barker R.T. | Driver | 03/09/25 | 13/10/41 | |
| Campbell B.J. | Driver | 19/10/28 | 15/02/43 | |
| Campbell T.P.M. | Driver | 28/01/21 | 01/04/40 | |
| Calland G. | Fireman | 07/10/43 | 14/05/62 | |
| Catterall W. | Passed Fireman | 04/08/39 | 25/03/57 | |
| Charnley L. | Fireman | 13/01/47 | 14/05/62 | |
| Chatwin D. | Fireman | 04/09/46 | 09/01/62 | |
| Claybrooke J. | Driver | 06/07/36 | 20/07/51 | |
| Clayton G. | Passed Fireman | 02/02/37 | 27/07/53 | |
| Clayton J. | Passed Fireman | 23/06/40 | 18/07/55 | |
| Clayton J.P. | Fireman | 03/12/46 | 18/03/63 | |
| Clough R. | Driver | 23/08/29 | 11/06/45 | |
| Commons V | Driver | 26/04/28 | 19/08/42 | |
| Commons W.J. | Driver | 12/10/24 | 28/07/42 | |
| Cooper J.R. | Driver | 22/07/18 | 21/01/37 | |
| Cooper S.E. | Driver | 13/04/21 | 14/08/39 | |
| Craghill E. | Driver | 23/04/04 | 24/06/18 | Shunting only – medical grounds |
| Crimp M.E. | Fireman | 21/08/45 | 21/10/62 | |
| Critchley T. | Driver | 07/10/03 | 08/04/18 | |
| Cumming R. | Passed Fireman | 19/07/39 | 09/08/54 | |
| Dixon H. | Driver | 23/01/18 | 01/07/37 | |
| Doyle P. | Driver | 25/06/27 | 25/10/49 | |
| Edge E.A. | Driver | 17/02/30 | 26/06/50 | |
| Eyers G.E. | Fireman | 17/04/46 | 01/04/63 | |
| Fenner D. | Driver | 06/11/24 | 22/03/48 | |
| Finney H.F. | Driver | 06/06/30 | 03/05/48 | |
| Fletcher J.T. | Fireman | 23/12/46 | 05/02/62 | |
| Fletcher P.W. | Driver | 14/04/32 | 28/03/49 | |
| Fletcher R.R. | Fireman | 18/10/45 | 30/07/62 | |
| Ford G. | Passed Fireman | 02/06/40 | 08/08/55 | |
| Forshaw D.H.M. | Passed Cleaner | 03/10/51 | 28/03/67 | |
| Fowler H.T. | Passed Fireman | 24/11/43 | 21/08/61 | |
| Gillett W.A. | Passed Fireman | 11/04/39 | 02/01/61 | |
| Gorton D. | Fireman | 20/02/47 | 07/05/62 | |
| Grimshaw P.H. | Fireman | 28/08/45 | 25/06/62 | |
| Guest R. | Fireman | 29/06/47 | 07/08/62 | |
| Hall A.S. | Passed Fireman | 08/08/40 | 15/08/55 | |

| Name | Grade | D.O.B | Seniority Date | Remarks |
|------|-------|-------|----------------|---------|
| Hall N. | Driver | 29/03/04 | 06/09/20 | |
| Hall R. | Driver | 20/11/19 | 19/11/35 | |
| Halliwell D. | Passed Fireman | 06/08/44 | 09/10/61 | |
| Halsall W.M. | Fireman | 10/10/47 | 08/01/63 | |
| Harney F. | Driver | 04/10/30 | 12/05/47 | |
| Hartnett M.R.G. | Passed Fireman | 14/03/44 | 26/03/62 | |
| | Fireman | 28/08/45 | 16/04/62 | |
| Hawley C. | Driver | 16/05/35 | 14/08/50 | |
| Heald R.J. | Passed Cleaner | 27/12/49 | 03/10/66 | |
| Heardman F. | Driver | 25/09/30 | 22/08/49 | |
| Hesketh G.K. | Driver | 20/02/18 | 24/02/37 | |
| Heyes E. | Driver | 15/02/35 | 17/04/50 | |
| Higham S. | Driver | 09/08/23 | 01/04/41 | |
| Hogg I.P. | Passed Fireman | 29/09/43 | 03/04/61 | |
| Hopkinson F. | Driver | 26/06/19 | 14/06/37 | |
| Howard J. | Driver | 08/08/27 | 06/09/43 | |
| Hutchinson C.D. | Fireman | 31/07/35 | 27/08/62 | |
| Johnston P. | Driver | 06/01/23 | 17/02/47 | |
| Jones A. | Driver | 02/03/30 | 22/05/44 | |
| Jones T.E. | Fireman | 14/01/50 | 23/08/65 | |
| Kay R. | Driver | 10/02/06 | 20/06/22 | |
| Marlor J.E. | Fireman | 20/01/47 | 10/06/63 | |
| Marsden A.R. | Fireman | 17/07/48 | 31/08/65 | |
| McFadyen B.L. | Driver | 01/06/35 | 24/07/50 | |
| Mcnamara J. | Driver | 22/03/24 | 23/12/40 | |
| Moss James. | Driver | 07/05/17 | 01/03/37 | |
| Moulding H. | Driver | 03/03/08 | 15/02/27 | Local shunt & trip duties – medical grounds. |
| Myers B.R. | Passed fireman | 23/05/35 | 25/04/57 | |
| Neele T. | Driver | 23/02/25 | 12/09/46 | |
| Nelson C. | Driver | 15/08/18 | 17/03/36 | |
| Newham D. | Passed Cleaner | 19/03/51 | 28/12/66 | |
| Norris P.R. | Driver | 22/06/36 | 16/07/51 | |
| Nowell W. | Passed Fireman | 07/12/39 | 19/02/62 | |
| Parker J. | Driver | 23/01/18 | 01/07/37 | |
| Parker S.H. | Driver | 28/03/22 | 31/03/41 | |
| Parkinson R. | Fireman | 06/04/50 | 02/08/65 | |
| Peet D.T. | Passed Fireman | 29/08/44 | 08/05/61 | |
| Pirie G. | Driver | 12/06/30 | 15/05/50 | |
| Pollard D.G. | Passed Fireman | 08/01/41 | 17/07/61 | |
| Potter C. | Passed Fireman | 13/01/41 | 10/01/57 | |
| Ridley R.S. | Fireman | 25/05/47 | 13/08/62 | |
| Rigby M.P. | Fireman | 13/12/46 | 08/01/62 | |
| Roach J.W. | Fireman | 20/01/47 | 27/08/62 | |
| Robinson H. | Passed Fireman | 08/11/39 | 09/01/56 | |
| Sargeant J.W. | Fireman | 18/06/47 | 20/01/64 | |
| Scard R.G. | Fireman | 21/12/46 | 29/10/62 | |
| Scott A. | Driver | 18/12/18 | 11/05/36 | |
| Sewell D.G. | Passed Fireman | 30/07/44 | 04/12/61 | |
| Shaw C. | Driver | 13/02/24 | 01/01/41 | |

| Name | Grade | D.O.B | Seniority Date | Remarks |
|---|---|---|---|---|
| Simons W. | Driver | 04/02/04 | 20/08/18 | Diesel shunts only – medical grounds |
| Smith A. | Fireman | 05/06/47 | 24/07/62 | |
| Spiby M.W. | Fireman | 17/01/46 | 12/07/65 | |
| Stewart D. | Passed Cleaner | 26/08/46 | 28/12/66 | |
| Stuart C.F. | Driver | 11/10/05 | 21/03/24 | Shed yard limits on steam locos. - medical grounds. |
| Tanton W.G.S | Driver | 10/12/23 | 14/07/47 | |
| Taylor W.H. | Driver | 17/03/25 | 30/06/41 | |
| Thomas R. | Driver | 07/08/24 | 14/09/42 | |
| Thompson S.P. | Fireman | 17/03/50 | 26/07/65 | |
| Thomson G. | Passed Cleaner | 22/10/51 | 04/04/67 | |
| Tingley A.G. | Passed Cleaner | 09/10/43 | 28/11/66 | |
| Tomlinson R. | Driver | 02/03/30 | 25/05/45 | |
| Tuson J.P. | Fireman | 07/07/45 | 31, 08. 65 | |
| Unsworth J. | Passed Fireman | 23/11/38 | 12/03/56 | |
| Walkden B.D. | Passed Fireman | 12/03/39 | 20/04/54 | |
| Wall G.E. | Driver | 21/04/30 | 08/04/46 | |
| Wareing R. | Driver | 11/06/17 | 05/10/36 | |
| Wells F.J. | Driver | 09/07/24 | 09/05/49 | |
| Westwood D. | Passed Fireman | 05/06/41 | 07/08/56 | |
| Whalley J. | Driver | 27/11/32 | 11/04/49 | |
| Whyte J. | Fireman | 08/05/46 | 04/12/61 | |
| Wilcock J.P. | Fireman | 30/11/74 | 07/01/63 | |
| Wilding D. | Passed Fireman | 07/11/34 | 05/09/55 | |
| Wilson W. | Driver | 09/10/17 | 26/03/34 | |
| Yeowart R.J. | Fireman | 11/12/47 | 13/09/65 | |

## Staff list of shed conciliation grades for Lostock Hall M.P.D.

| Name | Grade | D.O.B | Seniority Date | Remarks |
|---|---|---|---|---|
| Allison W. | Shedman | 22/11/99 | 26/03/20 | Retained over age 65 |
| Bailey J. | Foreman's assistant class2 | 13/01/16 | 31/05/37 | |
| Bamford T. | Ldg. Shedman (Stores issuer) | 27/04/13 | 12/04/48 | |
| Batt F.R. | Shedman | 19/03/04 | 08/01/68 | Ex-workshop grades 8.1.68-medical D.E.S 27-6-55. |
| Bolton H. | Leading Shedman (Telephone Attendant) | 23/09/21 | 08/04/46 | (Footplate) transferred to Shed Staff 28. 3. 66 – medical grounds. |
| Brown H. | Ldg. Shedman (C.P. Attd.) | 09/04/16 | 12/06/61 | |
| Cross T.L. | Shedman | 26/02/02 | 22/10/51 | Retained over age 65. |
| Dickson R.G. | Shedman | 11/05/11 | 20/09/65 | |
| Dixon R.F. | Senior Shedman (Boilerwasher) | 11/01/17 | 07/02/55 | |
| Dolan T. | Senior Shedman (Steamraiser) | 17/10/22 | 07/11/57 | |
| Dolan T. (Jnr.) | Shedman | 19/12/45 | 06/06/66 | |
| Fazackerley D.G. | Shedman | 30/12/45 | 28/11/66 | |
| Forrest T. | Senior Shedman (Boilerwasher) | 29/12/35 | 28/05/56 | |
| Green H. | Shedman | 07/07/00 | 24/11/19 | Retained over age 65 |

| Name | Grade | D.O.B | Seniority Date | Remarks |
|------|-------|-------|----------------|---------|
| Hughes V.J. | Foreman's Assistant. Class 2 | 26/10/26 | 02/02/48 | (Footplate) transferred to Shed Staff 12. 9. 60 – medical grounds. |
| Johnson W.R. | Shedman | 13/09/02 | 21/09/20 | Retained over age 65 |
| Layden B.F. | Senior Shedman (Steamraiser) | 26/07/31 | 21/02/61 | |
| Mayor J. | Leading Shedman (Stores Issuer) | 01/12/23 | 07/01/47 | (Footplate) transferred to Shed Staff 6. 5. 47 – medical. |
| Morris C.E. | Foreman's Assistant Class 2 | 28/04/24 | 07/03/41 | (Footplate) transferred to Shed Staff 12. 12. 66 – medical grounds |
| Parker B. | Shedman | 22/03/38 | 14/04/53 | (Footplate) transferred to Shed Staff 24. 9. 62. Technical exam for driving. |
| Perry W. | Leading Shedman (Stores Issuer) | 16/10/06 | 12/05/46 | |
| Robinson W. | Chargeman Cleaner | 07/05/17 | 25/11/35 | (Footplate) transferred to Shed Staff 6. 2. 39 – medical grounds. |
| Sharples K.F. | Shedman | 01/11/20 | 27/10/52 | (Footplate) transferred to Shed Staff 17. 08. 53 at own request |
| Weasingham A. | Shedman | 01/10/22 | 22/04/66 | |
| Woan J. | Senior Shedman (Steamraiser) | 02/08/17 | 20/01/47 | |
| Underwood F.J. | Shedman | 26/03/01 | 19/04/60 | Retained over age 65. |

Retired Preston driver, Walter (Rocky) Thompson, related a tale about Bob Cunningham who was the last shed-master prior to the closure in 1961. He was awarded the nick-named, Bob Hope, because he looked like the entertainer and had the same subtle sense of humour: *"Patriot class loco, 45519 Lady Godiva, was supposed to have been cleaned one day, prior to working the 8. 15 to Windermere, but the fireman's side next to the shed's east wall was left undone. Mr. Cunningham inspected the clean side of the engine only, and patted the buffer beam saying, "That's my grand old lady". When she returned to the shed that afternoon, she was facing south, this time with the fireman's side next to the west wall, which didn't matter anyway, because Mr. Cunningham had gone home!"*

Walter went on to explain that when those working on the permanent way were in need of coal for the stove, they would stand by the track with out-stretched arms, as if begging for Alms. On seeing this one day, Walter heaved a huge cob out of the tender onto the footplate. He had plenty of time, as the engine was going through a speed restriction. On approaching the men, he shoved the cob off the footplate with his boot, but as it hit the ground, it spun off to the right and smashed through the wooden wall of the plate-layers' hut. Men came running out in all directions!

Retired driver Tony Gillett recalled the story of the driverless train: *"One day I was firing for Paul Jameson (later a footplate inspector) on a special from the Crewe area to Blackpool. Anyway, it turned out that we had both been reading one of Norman McKillop's books, in which the engine crew had taken refuge in the tender, with a view to spooking a signalman. Both Paul and myself must have been in a 'silly half hour' mood because we decided to emulate the suggested footplate technique at Wigan, where we were booked to pick up passengers. The locomotive was a 'Crab' 2-6-0 ; the cab of which was the more exposed to public view owing to the tender being narrower than the engine. I hid myself in the tender while Paul adopted a kneeling position on the footplate so he could manipulate the controls and just see where he was going. We swept into the platform and stopped, looked at each other and had a good laugh, but our merriment was cut short when loco inspector Arthur King was seen stalking up the platform with a face like thunder. Now whatever inspector King's undoubted virtues were, an ebullient sense of humour was not high on the score sheet. This was going to be a severe reprimand matter, if not a suspension. Arthur King (always referred to as King Arthur by enginemen) came to the engine, glared at the pair of us, looked us both up and down, then observed, "Hmm, right bundles of fun today, aren't we?"; then broke into a beaming smile and sauntered off down the platform; and not another word was said. I still wonder what glad tidings had brought on this sudden change of character!"*

The last surviving Super D's at Preston, 49104 and 49408, on June 13, 1963. (*Bob Watkins*)

Farewell with a bit of black humour. This is how the fitter's shop looked following closure on October 10, 1961. *(Tony Gillett)*

KItson saddle-tank, 48008, on the pits, June 17, 1961. She was used for shunting on the short-radiused curves at Green Bank, and had to be towed there and back from the shed, as her short wheel-base didn't always register on the track-circuit system. *(Tony Gillett)*

Bob Tye related a story about a retired railwayman whose back garden terminated close to the Fylde line at Ashton. He devised a novel method of getting free coal by erecting a scare-crow next the the fence and placing an old top hat on its head. The sea-side bound footplate crews would have a go at knocking the top hat off with cobs as they passed by. They never managed to hit the target, but the old man never went short of fuel.

The beginning of the end came on June 28th, 1960, when the timber roof caught fire. 13 locomotives were trapped inside, of which those allocated to the shed were, Stanier Mogul, 42945; Black 5's, 45150 and 45315; Royal Scot, 46161, King's Own; Super D 0-8-0's, 49104, 49382 and 49396; Standard class 2, 78037. Visiting locomotives included Crab 2-6-0, 42707, from Fleetwood; Black 5, 54065 from Aston; Jubilee, 45675, Hardy, from Leeds Holbeck; Stanier 8F, 48414, from Toton and Standard 4-6-0, 73128, from Patricroft.

Royal Scot, 46168, The Girl Guide, on August 8, 1964. *(S.L. Pogmore)*

Once the fire was out, the locomotives were moved to Maudland goods yard across the way, and later on, all of them, save 49396, were taken to the workshops for repairs, cleaning and repainting.

The cause of the fire had been attributed to a Super D locomotive which was being prepared in the shed for a trip on the Pilling Pig; Jack Cray was stoking her up, but there was a considerable amount of coal dust in the tender and it came out of the chimney in a volcano of sparks, setting fire to the roof.

The charred wreckage was cleaned up, buckled rails replaced and temporary motive power was allocated in place of the damaged engines. The staff struggled on at the roofless building for another 13 months, under what can only be described as appalling conditions, until it was finally closed on September 12th, 1961. The locomotives and men were transferred to other depots, including Lostock Hall, Blackpool and Wigan, and the derelict structure remained standing for another 4 years until it was demolished in September, 1965. It is rumoured that the reason for the delay in the closure of the shed following the fire, was due to a retirement issue, involving Joe (Jimmy) Turner, the long-serving Lostock Hall shed master, who didn't like the idea of 'North Union' men joining the staff while he was still in charge there. He retired in September 1961, and his place was taken by Harold Sedgebeer, who pulled the signal off for the N.U. men to enter the yard. It is also said of Mr. Turner, that he turned down the offer of four brand new Crab, 2-6-0 locomotives, because he was quite content with his collection of antique L.Y. R. specimens.

B.R. (L.M.R.)                        WESTERN DIVISION.                    ERO.46857

                FREIGHT ENGINE WORKING : COMMENCED SEPTEMBER 26th, 1949.

                ENGINE WORKINGS ONLY.              PRESTON - SHEET 36.
                                                   (Reissued 14.11.49).
Turn 300.
                        NOT USED


_____

                        ONE CLASS 7F. (LNW 0-8-0).

Turn 301.                        No.12 Trip

SX    L.E.      8.30 am Shed              N.U. Yard          8.35
SX    Frt.      9.0    N.U. Yard          Lostock Hall       9.15    (590)
SX    Frt.      9.25   Lostock Hall       Preston E.L.       9.35
SX    E&B      10.10   Preston E.L.       Lostock Hall      10.23
SX    Frt.     10.50   Lostock Hall       Ribble Sdgs.      11.5
SX    Frt.     11.42   Ribble Sdgs.       Maudland          11.52
SX    Frt.     12.20 pm Maudland          Courtaulds        12.40
SX    Frt.      1.10   Courtaulds         Farington Jn. SL   1.45
SX    Frt.      2.50   Farington Jn.SL.   Leyland            2.57
SX    Frt.      2.57   SHUNT              Leyland            6.35    (591)
SX    Frt.      6.35   Leyland            Farington Jn.      6.45
SX    Frt.      7.15   Farington Jn.      Ribble Sdgs.       7.25
SX    L.E.      7.30   Ribble Sdgs.       Greenbank          7.38
SX    Frt.      8.10   Greenbank          N.U. Yard          8.17
SX    L.E.      8.55   N.U. Yard          Farington Jn.      9.5
SX    L.E       9.20   Farington Jn.      Shed               9.30

SO    T.F.      6.25 am Preston           Heysham            9.27 (  597)
SO    L.E.      -      Heysham            Carnforth Shed     -

SO    E.F.(MC) 11.10 pm Carnforth         Patricroft        2.23 am (10A/752.716)
Sun.  L.E. as reqd - Patricroft           Preston            -      (11A/434)


_____


Turn 302.
                        NOT USED.

_____


Turn 303.                        ONE CLASS 5 (STD. 4-6-0).
                                 Also Works Turns 32 and 33.
SX    E.F.      5.50 pm Preston           Warrington         7.55    (596)
MX    FF2       3.40 am (Warrington       Preston R.S.       4.40 (8B/602)(208)
                        (9.15pm from Camden.

_____


Turns 304 to 313.
                        NOT USED.

_____


            PRESTON LOCO' DEPOT to acknowledge receipt of this sheet by
                wire to "TRAINS P.E. CREWE" using the wording
                        "SHEET  546 "


                                                                        155

Ex L.N.W. 4-6-0 No. 8852, at Ashton on July 1, 1933. *(L. Hanson)*

# CHAPTER SIX

# Maudland, Green Bank & Oxheys

## Maudland Goods

The Maudland area as seen from the sky in the early 1930's. *(British Railways)*

### Extracts from structural survey carried out by author on July 28, 1992

Following the closure and dismantling of the Preston & Wyre crossing in 1885 and the construction of the Longridge branch curve in the same year, the layout at Maudland comprised a L.N.W. warehouse, cattle dock, six coal sidings and a siding for the Steam Saw Company. A water tank building and water-softening plant, which served the siphons at the engine shed across the tracks, were located in the north-west corner of the yard adjacent to the stables. In the 1850's, a coal yard and sidings were built on the east side of the Lancaster line, between the Pedder Street and Fylde Road bridges. The yard was closed and removed in 1884 and replaced with a large water-tank building. Most of the yard area was paved with Longridge stone setts, and they appeared to have stood the test of time very well. The standard size for these was 6"x 5"x 5", with trimming setts of various sizes, the most common of these being 5"x 3" x 5". It must have been fascinating to have observed the process of construction here. The work commenced with levelling out and setting up cambers and slopes, with the ground being cut away to the required depth. As these operations were taking place, the masons, on site and at the stone yard at Deepdale, would have been busy cutting the blocks to size. Next was the painstaking task of laying each sett in its proper place, tamping it down with a F.B.M. (fairly big mallet) and checking for continuity. Once the

Plan of Maudland area, 1892. *(Harris Library)*

master paver was satisfied with the way it looked, the spaces between the setts were partly filled in with cinders, blinded with sand and compacted. The work was then completed by filling in the remaining spaces with molten tar, using the hot bucket and ladle method. Only small sections at a time were completed in order to avoid calamities.

The two-storey warehouse was completed in 1885, on what was roughly the site of the old P&WR engine shed. It handled mainly cotton and engineering merchandise as well as agricultural produce from the Longridge area.

The interior of the building was served by a single straight-through track, terminating at a wagon turntable at the west end, which was connected to a parallel siding on the south side by way of a second turntable. An interior platform ran the full length of the north side, and was served by two loading bays with slated canopies. The offices and weigh bridge were located to the rear of the building. The main walls were 29 inches thick and made up for the most part with Accrington, Nori double-frogged red bricks, in English Garden bond, with one header to every three stretcher courses. The reveals on the loading bays and external hoists were trimmed at the corners with blue bull-nosed engineering bricks. There was an external jigger hoist on the east elevation and another in the centre of the north elevation. Each had a small drop-down platform on the first floor bay, which was secured to the wall by means of two lengths of chain in the manner of a tailgate. This was to allow the operator an extra bit of 'reach' beneath the cat head, and I often wonder if he got any danger money for standing on it.

The first floor comprised 12" x 3" thick pine boards with iron-trimmed tongue and grooved joints, laid on H-section transverse steel girders. In addition to the two external hoists, there were five serving the interior, three of which were located directly over the through track on the south side, and two above the platform on the north side. Only three of these jiggers retained their original L.N.W.R. number plates, 2959/60/61, with lifting capacities of between 5 and 10 cwt.

158

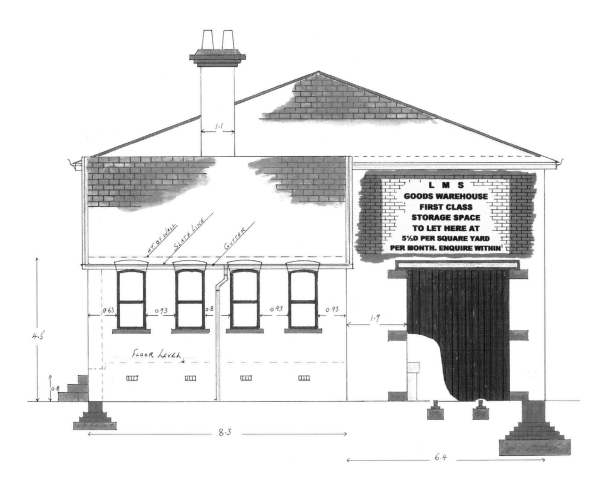

West elevation. *(Author)*

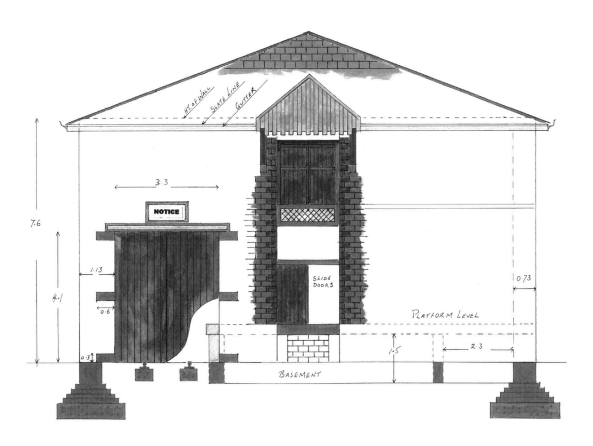

East elevation. *(Author)*

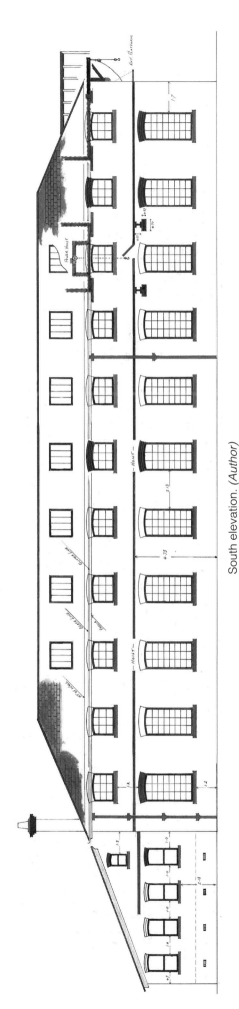

South elevation. (Author)

North elevation. (Author)

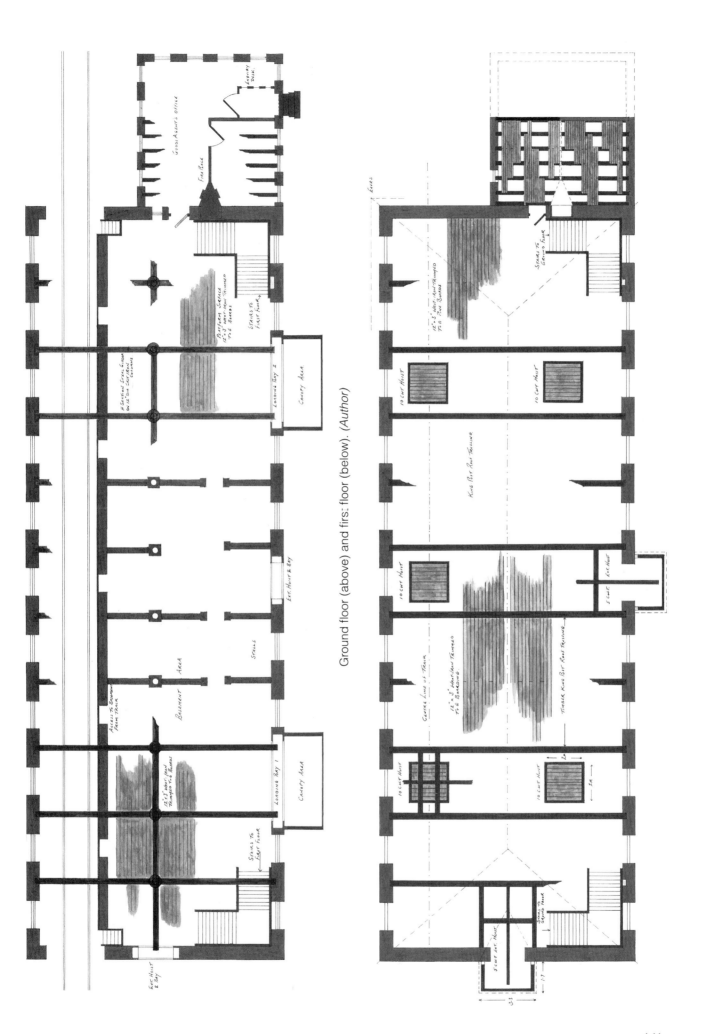

Ground floor (above) and first floor (below). (Author)

View from the south-east. February 15, 1992. *(Author)*

View from the north west. February 15, 1992. *(Author)*

The building continued to operate under L.M.S ownership as a transit warehouse until 1930, when its role was changed to that of a private storage warehouse. The adjacent cattle pens to the north of the building and stables fell into disuse at around the same time. The company's terms of storage were to be clearly seen on the west wall above the track entrance, and the advertisement was so placed as to catch the attention of those on passing trains. The wording, painted in black against a cream background read, 'L.M.S. GOODS WAREHOUSE. FIRST CLASS STORAGE SPACE TO LET AT 5 ½ D PER SQUARE YARD PER MONTH. ENQUIRE WITHIN.' The words remained just about legible to the very end. Storage facilities were withdrawn by B.R. in the late 50's when the building was leased to the first of two coal merchants, the ground floor being used only as a lock-up for the merchant's delivery wagons and conveyance machinery. The rest of the building including the offices was allowed to fall into a state of dereliction. Coal delivery to the premises by rail was discontinued in the early 70's, when it became less expensive to move things by road. The coal merchant proudly proclaimed that during the colliery strikes of 1984, over 300 tons of coal had been stored on the first floor. The stout boards in the main building were able to withstand the great weight, but this was not the case with the office buildings, where the overspill had proved too much for the lighter timbers, hence the collapsed masonry on the south wall. There was a basement of sorts with bricked-up lights beneath the loading platform. Access was by way of a trapdoor, with very limited room to move about.

Stock-piles of coal and anthracite, rotting timbers and missing slates.
A building waiting to die. September 13, 1989. *(Author)*

The warehouse was gutted by fire on July 29, 1992, just 24 hours after the structural survey had been carried out. It broke out around 16.30 hrs., when sparks from oxy-acetylene equipment came into contact with combustible material. The fire flared up and spread rapidly; the men were unable to bring it under control, so they called in the brigade and got clear of the building, which was a veritable tinder box, with all that dry timber, coal dust and Diesel oil. The whole building was well ablaze before the brigade arrived, and it took tenders from 4 other fires services to bring it under control. For the second time in 32 years all main line traffic was brought to a stand-still at Preston, owing to a huge fire on railway property at Maudland. Demolition on the burned-out shell commenced on August 11, 1992 and was completed three days later. It was the last of Preston's railway goods warehouses to disappear, the others being, Christian Road (L.N.W); Deepdale (P&L.R.); Butler Street (E.L.R); Butler Street (L.Y. R); Fishergate Hill (W.L.R) and the two sheds at Green Bank (L.N.W.).

Night of the fire, July 29, 1992. *(Author)*

Ex-L.N.W. Loco, 5761 (formerly 4202) at Maudland on May 28, 1927. *(W. H. Whitworth)*

Hughes 4-6-0, 10449, passes number 5 box with a train of mixed stock for Blackpool. The tank-wagon might have been attached as a precaution in the light of water shortages in the Fylde area. (*Author's collection*)

What it was all about in those golden days: good, clean fun by the track side. Jubilee, 45724, Warspite, provides the entertainment for a group of enthusiastic youngsters (and an adult) on July 1, 1961. *(Tony Gillett)*

L.N.W.R. cast-iron bridge plate on the abutment of Leighton Street bridge. *(Tony Gillett)*

Manufacturer's nameplate on the north parapet of the canal bridge. July 27, 1992. *(Author)*

Postcard of St. Walburg's, with Maudland goods yard on the left. *(Author's collection)*

Jubilee, 45601, British Guiana, reverses past the Longridge junction
on June 14, 1961. *(Tony Gillett)*

The name Maudland is derived from the middle English word, Maudelein or Magdalene or Magdalen. Saint Walburg's church was built close to the site of Saint Mary's Leper Hospital, and the magnificent slender spire continues to dominate the town's northern horizon. The church stands between the Lancaster and Blackpool lines, at the junction of Pedder and Weston Street, and the limestone spire, which reaches a height of 300 ft. is the third highest in the land and the highest for any church, the other two being cathedrals. The church was designed by the architect, Joseph Hansom (of Hansom cab fame), and erected by the Preston contractors, Cooper & Tullis in 1854. Sandstone was used on the main building, and the spire, which was completed in 1867, was made from limestone, as the base for the tower had been constructed using redundant limestone sleeper blocks from the Lancaster & Preston Railway. In the early years, railway and industrial communities made up a large portion of the congregation, which continued well into the 20th century, when they were uprooted, divided and dispersed to other areas of the town in the wake of the disastrous social engineering programmes of the 1960's and 70's.

Patriot, 45542, and Jubilee, 45700, Amethyst, making easy work of a heavy express. *(Tony Gillett)*

Fireman's view of Maudland from the footplate of Jubilee, 45629, Straits Settlements, on May 20, 1962. *(Tony Gillett)*

168

Patriot, 45515, Caernarvon, accelerates past Stanier class 4 tank, 42461, with steam to spare, on June 14, 1961. *(Tony Gillett)*

Fowler 4MT tank, 42379, hurries south with a North Eastern carriage on July 1, 1961. *(Tony Gillett)*

The first of the recorded railway fires at Maudland, and perhaps the only one to have a happy ending, occurred on Tuesday, January 15, 1850. A night watchman at the P&W station discovered a fire in the adjoining engine shed in the early hours of the morning, and notified the nearby Police Station, whereupon a huge fire-bell was rung. Within a few minutes, the 'Victoria' and 'Prince of Wales' fire engines arrived at the location of a fire-plug on Maudland Bank; the water pressure at this point, however, was found to be too low, but the resourceful men procured a plentiful supply of water from the pipe which served the locomotive siphons, and within two hours the fire had been extinguished. There was only one engine in the shed at that time and, apart from the paintwork being blistered,

Another impressive view of Maudland, with too much detail to mention. The premises of the Steam Saw Mill Co. are clearly illustrated in the centre of the picture, with siding and overhead gantry. The ironwork for Leighton Street bridge (bridge No. 1) was manufactured by J. C. Clayton, Soho Foundry, Preston in 1847. *(British Railways Board)*

46242, City of Glasgow, passes Maudland yard in 1961. *(Tony Gillett)*

she remained undamaged. Fortuitously, the fire broke out at the west end of the building, for had it originated at the other end, there would have been much more serious damage, as the east end was adjoined by a stable in which were kept two fine horses. The beneficial effects of keeping horses at the Fire Brigade Station were plainly shown at this particular fire, for without them the engines could not have been conveyed to the spot in anything like the time occupied on this occasion, and thus the fire might have obtained much greater head before assistance was at hand. [1]

Ale houses in the area included the Maudland Inn, proprietress Margaret Grime in 1873; Telegraph Inn, proprietress Elizabeth Howard in 1872 and the Union Hotel, Maudland Bank. Proprietor Mr. T. Swindlehurst in 1875.

45712, Victory, at Maudland on July 1, 1961. *(Tony Gillett)*

The Preston steam-powered breakdown crane with attendant tool vans and carriages,
at Maudland on February 21, 1961. *(Tony Gillett)*

Post-steam view of the north gantry.
(Authors Collection)

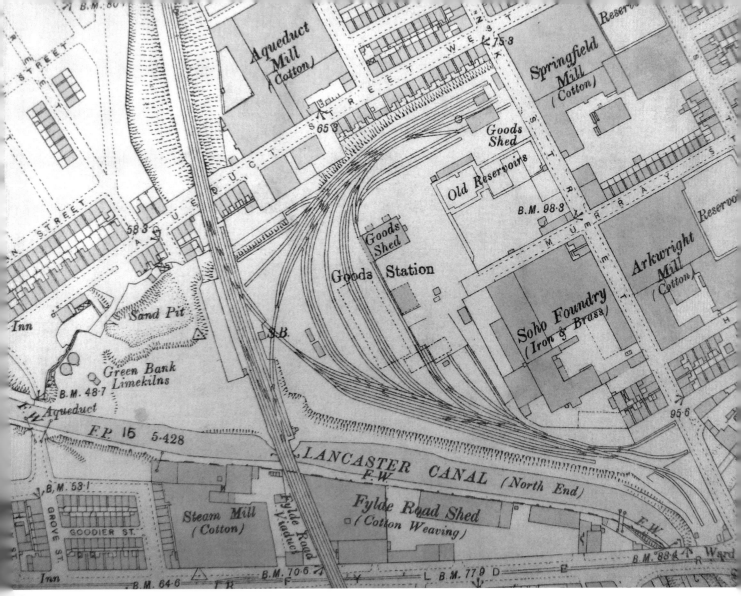

1892 plan of Green Bank sidings. *(Harris Library)*

# Green Bank

The yard at Green Bank comprised two small goods sheds and a travelling crane, and was another of those railway sites in Preston, where much had to be crammed into little. It was located on the east side of the Lancaster line and served by branches from the up and down tracks. The main client here was Foster's Soho Foundry, which specialised in large industrial boilers, hence the overhead crane. Other manufacturers in the immediate area included the Arkwright, Springfield and Aqueduct mills. A loading platform was built for the Green Bank lime kilns, which continued to send their products north by way of the canal. Such was the severity of the curves, that only 4-coupled engines were allowed to work there. The shunters had to be piloted to Green Bank from Preston and back, owing to the propensity of the short wheel-bases failing to register on the track-circuit system. The site was originally owned by the Green Bank Branch Railway Company, the agents for whom were Myers, Veevers and Myers of 15 Chapel Street, Preston.

It is interesting to note that during the course of the Galgate Bridge inquiry at Lancaster Assizes, in July, 1839, George Stephenson stated that he was one of the first engineers to build skew bridges, and had built several of them on the Liverpool & Manchester Railway. He added that the necessity of avoiding short curves on railways had suddenly brought these singular constructions into common use; and that they were generally considered to have originated with the railways. The proprietors of the Lancaster Canal, however, believed that the first skew bridge in England was built by their resident engineer, William Cartwright, on their canal upwards of forty years before, and that the location of this bridge was stated to be Green Bank, where the Fylde Road crossed the canal. [2]

173

Aerial photo of Green Bank. *(British Railways Board)*

Green Bank Goods memo to Grange, 1916. *(Author's collection)*

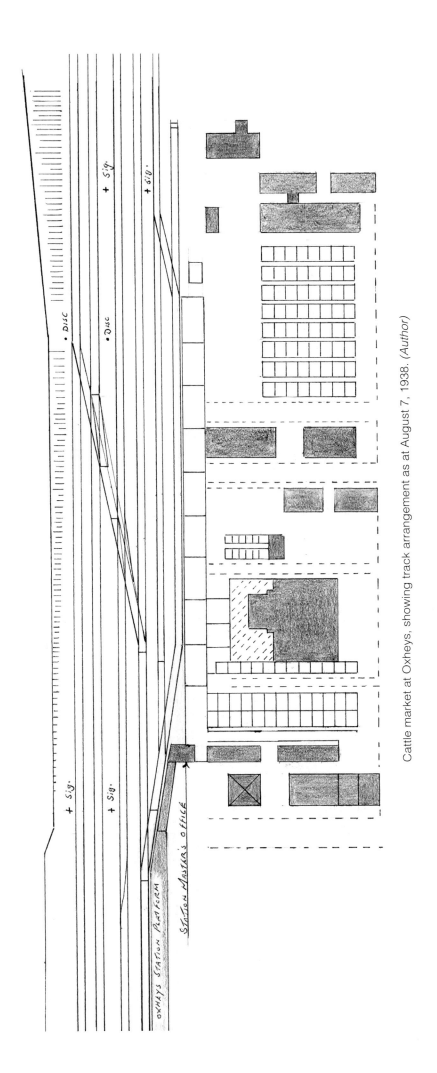

Cattle market at Oxheys, showing track arrangement as at August 7, 1938. (Author)

175

Oxheys looking north, with the newly completed by-pass bridge. *(Harris Library)*

Oxheys by-pass bridge under construction. *(Harris Library)*

## FOOTNOTES

(1) Preston Chronicle, January 19, 1850.

(2) Preston Chronicle, July 13, 1839.

# CHAPTER 7

# Miscellaneous

Johnson's Railway Watch advert, with illustrations. Mr. Johnson was a versatile man and a successful entrepreneur. He was first and foremost a reputable jeweller, specialising in railway time-pieces, then he adapted part of his premises in Orchard Street, Preston, for use as a parcels office for the L.N.W.R., working on a commission basis as an agent. It opened for business on July 23, 1870. He later opened a warehouse at 33 Lune Street for the sale of pianofortes and harmoniums. His son, John Johnson Junior, became an auctioneer and valuer and opened a premises at No. 13, Orchard Street.

*(Photo's: Mike Atherton)*

"HE THAT HAS A WATCH TWO THINGS MUST DO,
POCKET HIS WATCH AND WATCH HIS POCKET TOO"

## JOHN JOHNSON

### WHOLESALE AND RETAIL WATCH AND CLOCK MANUFACTURER

SILVERSMITH, WORKING JEWELLER, ENGRAVER, &C.,

11, 14 and 15 Orchard Street, Preston, Lancashire.

Specially Appointed

## WATCH MAKER TO THE ENGINE DRIVERS

On the London and North Western, London and South Western,
Great Western, Great Eastern, Great Northern, London, Chatham and Dover,
Lancashire and Yorkshire, Midland, Furness, Cambrian, Taff vale, Grand trunk,
Great Indian Peninsular, and East Indian railways.

### THE RAILWAY TIME-KEEPER AND BRITISH WORKMAN'S WATCH.

This article positively stands in the market without a rival, and cannot be equalled in the United Kingdom at the price. Ten thousand of them have been supplied to engine drivers on nearly every railway in the world. Description: best quality patent detached lever movement, jewelled in eight action in rubies, chronometer balances, sterling silver cases, twice the weight of ordinary cases, gold joints. Warranted to keep time to half a minute per week. All repairs free for three years after being purchased. **Price, only £5 5s.**

### THE RAILWAY GUARD'S WATCH.

This watch resembles externally those worn by railway guards, as it is fitted with a strong plate glass front, capable of resisting a great amount of violence before it can be broken. It thus combines the convenience of an open faced watch, with all the advantages, in point of strength, of a hunter; and as every care is taken in the construction of the movement, it is highly recommended to all persons who desire a watch of more than ordinary strength.
**Prices, £6 6s., £7 7s., £8.**

Gentlemen can have their **WATCHES REGULATED** to true time, free of cost,
by Johnson's patent compound Mercurial Regulating Chronometer.

Every known construction of English, French or Swiss
**CHRONOMETERS, REPEATERS,**
Duplex, Centre Seconds, Skeleton, Detached Lever, Horizontal or Verge Watches,
**REPAIRED, CLEANED AND ADJUSTED IN THE MOST SKILFUL MANNER.**
By our Efficient Staff of Practical Workers, **ON THE PREMISES.**

### BEST WATCH GLASSES IN THE TRADE NEATLY FITTED

And every other article in the trade at the most moderate prices.

### COMPATIBLE WITH FIRST CLASS WORKMANSHIP.

Punctuality is strictly observed, and Watches returned to the Owners within One Week.

**WATCHES, PLATE, JEWELRY, &c., FOR REPAIRS,**
Will meet with prompt and special attention from your obedient servant,

## JOHN JOHNSON.

# North Union Railway

*North Union Rule Book pertaining to Preston, for the year 1841:*

## Rules and Regulations

*To be observed by the* **NORTH UNION RAILWAY COMPANY,** *and by the Owners and Persons having the Care or Management and Conduct of Engines, Waggons, or Carriages, passing along or being upon the same, and by all parties using or working the said Railway; the Breach of any such Rules and regulations will subject the Offender to a Penalty of* **FIVE POUNDS,** *unless otherwise specified, besides such responsibility as may attach at Common Law.*

## 1

No moving Power shall be used, or be upon the Main Lines of Railway, between **Parkside** and **Preston,** except Locomotive Steam Engines.

## 11

No Locomotive Engine shall be used on the Railway, until approved of by the Company's Engineer or other Agent, except those which shall belong to, or be provided by any other Railway Company whose Road shall communicate with the Railway, and which Engines shall usually travel and be on the Road of such other Company; but every Person intending to use his own Locomotive Engine, shall give Notice in writing, to the Secretary of the Company, of such intention, stating some convenient place where such Engine may be inspected, whereupon the Company shall cause their Engineer or other Agent, within fourteen days from the Receipt of such Notice, to Inspect and Examine, and Report thereon, and within Seven days after such Reports Certificates shall be given, if required, stating whether such Engine is or is not fit to be used on the Railway; nevertheless, if such Party should be dissatisfied with the decision of the said Engineer or other Agent, he or they shall be at liberty to refer the sufficiency of such Locomotive Engine to Arbitration, under the 191st Section of the Act.

## 111

No Carriage for the Conveyance of Goods, Coal, Passengers, or Cattle, shall be permitted to pass along, or be upon the said railway, unless such carriage shall be approved of by the Engineer or other Agent of the Company authorised for that purpose; and every Owner of every Carriage or Waggon intended to be used for the Conveyance of Coal or Coke, or other articles usually weighed in the gross, shall cause (and is hereby required so to do) his or her Name, Place of Abode, Number, Weight, Painted and continued in large White Capital Letters and Figures on a Black Ground, and shall enter the same with the Secretary of the Company, or other Officer appointed for that purpose; and every Person who shall alter, erase, deface, or hide such Name, &c., or shall refuse to permit any Carriage to be Weighed, measured, or Gauged, whenever the Company's Officers shall, at the expense of the company, require to do so, shall forfeit and pay any sum not exceeding **FORTY SHILLINGS** for every such Offence.

## 1V

Every Engine, Waggon, and Carriage, being or working upon the Railway; and every Engineman. Fireman, breaksman, Waggoner, and every other Person belonging to, or attending the same, shall be under the direction and control of the Company and their Officers and Servants, as to the times of Starting, the Speed of travelling, ***and in all other respects,*** so far as may be necessary to secure despatch, and good order, and the safety of the Public.

# V

All Carriages and Trains composed of Carriages or Waggons laden with Goods or Coals shall get out of the way of any Passenger or Mail Train when required so to do, and shall immediately go and pass into such Sidings as shall be pointed out and directed by the Person or Persons in charge of, or conducting such Passenger or Mail Trains.

# V1

The Loading of any Waggon or Carriage shall not, in any case overhang the Rails on which such Waggons or Carriages is more than 18 inches on each side.

# V11

Every Train of Waggons not exceeding Five in number, shall be attended to by one Breaksman, and if the Train shall consist of more than Five, an additional Breaksman shall be appointed for every Five Waggons, and for every fractional part beyond Five complete.

# V111

No Locomotive Engine shall be allowed to propel any Waggon or Carriage upon or along the Railway, but shall in all cases draw the same after it.

# 1X

No Waggon laden with Coal, Stone, gravel, Goods or General Merchandise, shall be allowed to pass along the Railway on the Sabbath day.

# X

No Person except the Engineman and Fireman shall be allowed to ride on any Locomotive Engine or Tender upon or along the Railway, without the special licence of the Directors, in writing; and any Engineman so permitting any Person to ride, shall be fined FIVE SHILLINGS for every Offence. And no Person other than the Breaksman shall be allowed to pass free on any Goods, Coal, or Cattle Waggon.

# X1

No Person shall travel or pass on Foot along, or upon the Railway, or any Bridge thereof, over which the Railway is laid; and any Person using the Railway, or any such Bridge thereof, as a Foot-path, shall forfeit and pay any sum not exceeding FORTY SHILLINGS for every such Offence, and all Gate-keepers, Guards, Plate-layers, and others, Servants of the Company, are strictly enjoined and ordered to prevent and stop all Persons whatever from so offending.

# X11

No Person shall ride, lead, or drive, upon or along the Railway, any Horse, Mule or Ass, or any Cow, or other Neat Cattle, Sheep, Swine, or other beast or Animal; and every Person so offending shall forfeit and pay any sum not exceeding TEN POUNDS for every such Offence.

# X111

No Engine, Waggon, or Carriage, shall at any time be left upon the Main Lines of the Railway when not working.

## X1V

No Person whatsoever shall be allowed to smoke Tobacco in any First Class Carriage, or in, at, or upon any of the Stations, Waiting-Rooms, Booking-Offices, Wharfs, or Warehouses of the Company.

## XV

Every Engine, Tender, Waggon, or other Carriage, which shall, in the opinion of the Company's Engineer or other Officer appointed to inspect the same, become or be unsafe and unfit to be used on the Railway, shall immediately be removed from the Railway, upon orders to that effect being given by the Engineer or other Officer as aforesaid, either to the Owner or the person having charge of the same.

## XV1

No Locomotive Engine or Train of Carriages or Waggons, shall, under any pretence whatever, be allowed to pass along the wrong Line of Road, that is along the Eastern Line of railway in going towards *Preston,* or in a Northerly direction, or along the Western Line of Railway in going towards *Preston* in a Southerly direction.

## XV11

No Waggon or other Carriage shall, without consent, be loaded or unloaded while remaining on any part of the Main Lines of Way, except Carriages for the Conveyance of Passengers, stopping to take up or set down Passengers at any of the places appointed for that purpose; and all Carriages and Waggons, while at any of the Company's Stations, shall be under the control of the Company's Officers.

## XV111

No Persons shall be permitted to sell, or offer for sale, any Liquor, Beer, or other articles, upon the Line of Railway, or at any of the Stations; and all Guards, Policemen, Porters, and others, Servants of the Company, are strictly enjoined to remove every Person offending against this Bye-law, and immediately to give such information as will lead to the infliction of the Penalty for so doing.

## X1X

Any Passenger in a state of intoxication, committing any nuisance, or interfering with the comfort of other Passengers, or not attending to the directions of the Guard, in cases where the personal safety of himself, or any of the passengers is concerned, shall immediately, or so soon as the same can conveniently be done, be removed from the Company's Premises, without being entitled to have any part of the fare returned.

## XX

Any Servants of the Company accepting any Fee, Gratuity, or Reward, or asking or demanding such from any Passenger or other Person, for services rendered, or for any purpose whatsoever connected with the Railway, shall be instantly dismissed.

## XX1

The Drivers or Conductors of all Public Coaches, Omnibuses, or other Carriages, that may be admitted into the Company's Premises, shall obey every direction or order that may be given them by any of the Company's Agents or Servants, while on the said Premises; and every Driver or other Person refusing to obey such directions or orders, shall forfeit and pay the sum of TEN SHILLINGS for every such refusal.

*Given under the Common Seal of the* NORTH UNION RAILWAY, *this Fifth day of October, 1838.*

# North Union Railway

## Additional
## Rules and Regulations

*To be observed by the* **NORTH UNION RAILWAY COMPANY,** *and by the Owners or Persons having the care or Management and Conduct of Engines, Waggons, or Carriages, passing along or being upon the same, and by all Parties Using or Working the said Railway. The breach of any such Rules and Regulations will subject the Offender to a penalty of* **FIVE POUNDS,** *unless otherwise specified, besides each responsibility as may attach at Common Law.*

# XX11

Every private Railway joining to or connected with the Main Lines of the North Union Railway by means of Switches or moveable Points, shall be furnished with an Indicator (exhibiting a Gilt Arrow by day, and a Lamp by night), to show the position of the same, such Indicator to be kept locked down at all times when not in use; and such Railway or Siding shall also be furnished with a Stop Bar across the same, to be locked down when Waggons or other Carriages shall have passed in, such Indicators and Stop Bars to be made, set up, and placed under the directions of the Company's Engineers, but at the expense of the Owner or Owners of such private Railways.

# XX111

Every Owner of any private Railway or Siding connected with or joined to the said Railway, who shall leave the Switches wrong, or shall neglect the precautions of locking the Indicator, so as to prevent the same from being placed wrong, or shall leave the Stop Bar unlocked, shall be fined **FIVE POUNDS** for every such Offence; and in the event of any loss, damage, or accident taking place in consequence of such neglect, will be held responsible for the amount of the loss or damage so occasioned.

Given under the Common seal of the **NORTH UNION RAILWAY COMPANY,** the Ninth Day of January, One Thousand Eight Hundred and Forty.

# XX1V

Every Person desirous of bringing a Locomotive Engine on the Line of the **NORTH UNION RAILWAY,** shall give Notice in Writing of such intention to the Secretary of the Company, stating the place where such Engine can be seen, and the weight of the same together with the name of the Engine-man who is in charge and his ability and qualifications inquired into when, if no objection appears, a Certificate of permission will be granted for such Engine-man's Employment, when the Company's Rules and Regulations are to be read over and a copy of them to be furnished to him; and in case of such man leaving his place the like precautions are to be observed before the Employment of any new man in his place.

# XXV

No Coal Train shall leave the Siding where it may happen to be, until full Ten Minutes after the passing of the Train immediately preceding it, and no Coal Train shall upon any account come nearer than One Mile to the Train in motion before it, the observance of this Rule is particularly called for on the Inclines of one in a hundred, so that no two trains will in this case be on the incline descending together.

## XXV1

All Collier and Goods Engine-men are required to acquaint themselves with the times about which the Passenger Trains may be expected to pass their respective Sidings or Stations, and no Collier or Goods Engine must on any pretence come out on to or cross over the Line on which any Passenger Engine and Train is expected, within 15 minutes of the usual or ordinary time of the passing such place, and in the event of any accident occurring from the Neglect of this Regulation the Owners of such Engine will also be held strictly accountable for the damage that may ensue.

## XXV11

No Collier or Goods Train is to leave any Station whatever at a less interval of time than 20 minutes before the usual or ordinary time of the Passenger Trains passing the place where such Collier or Goods Train is to depart from.

## XXV111

All Collier and Goods Trains when likely to be overtaken by a Coach Train must use their best endeavours to get out of the way of the same by placing their own Trains in the nearest Siding, but in so doing especial care must be taken by blowing the whistle and sending back the Fireman or Breaksman to warn the coming Train (if after dusk, with a well-lighted red Signal Lamp) of what is going on.

## XX1X

Every Collier Engine shall have, between Sunset and Sunrise, a Light in front of the Engine, and One Large Red Light on the Rear Waggon of the Train.

## XXX

Every Engine-man or Fireman, of any Goods or Collier's Engine permitting any Person whosoever to ride or be on the Engine or Tender under their charge while passing along the Line, shall forfeit and pay to the Company the sum of TWENTY SHILLINGS for every person so permitted or carried, and for every such offence.

## XXX1

No Goods or Coal Trains shall be allowed to carry in any one Waggon a greater weight than Four Tons and the Coal or Slack, or other Articles carried loose, shall not be heaped up higher than 18 inches above the sides of the Waggons.

## XXX11

Bye-law No. 7 is hereby repealed, and instead thereof, it is ordered that every Coal or Goods Train shall have one Breaksman for any number of loaded Waggons not exceeding Nine; two Breaksmen for any number of Waggons exceeding Nine, and not exceeding Eighteen, three for any number of Waggons exceeding Eighteen, and not exceeding Twenty-seven, and so on; another Breaksman for every additional Nine Waggons.

## XXX111

Every Train passing on the Railway shall have the Carriages or Waggons of which it may be composed well coupled together with three good, substantial Coupling Chains; and it shall be the duty of every Engine-man, Fireman, breaksman and Guard, that may accompany such Train, to see that all three Coupling Chains are kept constantly and securely hooked when the Train is moving; and every Engine-man, Fireman, Breaksman and Guard neglecting this precaution shall be fined in any sum not exceeding TWENTY SHILLINGS each for every offence, each man being held alike responsible.

## XXX1V

The Breaksman of every Train passing on the Main Lines where only one attends a Train, shall always ride and be on the Last Waggon of the Train when moving, and where more than one breaksman attends a Train, one of them shall always be on the last Waggon; and in the event of the Breaksman being obliged unavoidably to leave such Waggon, the Break shall be pinned down before he quits it. The Plate-layers and others working on the Line, are required to report whenever the above rule is neglected; and any breaksman disregarding this regulation shall, on conviction, be fined any sum not exceeding TEN SHILLINGS for such offence.

## XXXV

If any Collier or Goods Train shall unavoidably stop on the Main Lines, the Engine-man of such Train, shall send back a trustworthy man, at least 400 Yards with a Red Flag by Day, and Good Light by Night to warn any coming train of such stoppage.

## XXXV1

Every Engine using the Railway shall proceed with the Engine before the Tender; and every Engine-man who shall unnecessarily and without sufficient cause run his Engine with the Tender in front, shall, on conviction, pay a penalty not exceeding TWENTY SHILLINGS for every such offence.

## XXXV11

No Engine or Train of any description shall pass through the **Preston** or **Wigan** Station while the Trains are stopping on the Main Lines, to set down or take up Passengers; and no Engine or Train shall pass through, or by the Station at Preston or Wigan at a greater speed that Six Miles per hour.

## XXXV111

The incline on the New Springs Branch being I in 30, particular attention is required to the following Regulations.

1st That no Locomotive Engine can be permitted to pass along the Line that is not fitted with a powerful Break, acting on the Two Driving Wheels on each side, in addition to a sufficient Break fitted to the Tender of such Engine, and to act on Four Wheels.

2nd That every Waggon using the Incline shall be fitted with a good, substantial Double Break and Strong Lever, and that every three loaded Waggons be attended by one Breaksman in the descent, who shall ride in the foremost Waggon down the incline, the other two Waggons shall have the Breaks pinned down.

3rd That no Train of Waggons or Engine shall commence to descend until the previous Train is clear of the incline.

4th No Engine or Waggon, whether full or empty, or other Carriage, shall, under any pretence whatever, be left standing on the Main Lines of the New Springs Branch Railway; and every owner of any Engine, Waggon, or other Carriage so left, shall be liable to a penalty of FIVE POUNDS for every such offence, half of which should be paid to the informer and the other half to the Company.

## XXX1X

No Locomotive Engine shall be used on the Railway exceeding in weight, in the whole, 15 tons; nor shall any Locomotive Engine be used having a greater weight on any one pair of wheels than Seven Tons.

*Given under the Common Seal of the* NORTH UNION RAILWAY COMPANY, *the Twenty-eighth Day of October, One Eight Thousand Hundred and Forty One.*

# Bibliography

**Nicholson, Peter.** A Popular and Practical Treatise on Masonry and Stone Cutting.

**Nicholson, Peter.** Guide to Railway Masonry, Containing a Complete Treatise on the Oblique Arch.

**Biddle, Gordon.** The Railways around Preston. An historical review. Foxline Publishing.

**Biddle, Gordon.** The Canals of North West England, Vol. 1. David & Charles.

**Reed, Brian.** Crewe to Carlisle. Ian Allan, 1969

**Barron, James.** History of Ribble Navigation. Preston Corporation, 1939

**British Railways Magazine.** London Midland Region July 1952, Vol. 3 No.7

**Web: Preston Station.** http://www.prestonstation.org.uk/

**Lostock Hall engine shed.** http://www.lostockhallmpd.org.uk/

**Dakres, Jack.** The Last Tide, A History of the Port of Preston. Carnegie Press.

**Railway Magazine.** 1960. Volume 106, parts 1, 2 and 3.

**Barritt S.** The Old Tram Road. Carnegie Publishing.

**Foster, R.** An introduction to Preston. Its History, Railways and Signalling. L.N.W.R. Society. Premier Portfolio No. 13.

**Fowler, A.** The Railways of Preston, Half a Century of Change. Atkinson Publications Ltd.

**Gregson, B.** The Lancashire and Yorkshire Railway around Preston. Atkinson Publications Ltd.

**Hindle, D. J.** Victorian Preston and the Whittingham Railway. Amberley Publishing.